The World Trade O

The World Trade Organization (WTO) is one of the most important international organizations in existence today. It contains a set of disciplines that affect the ability of governments to impose trade restrictions, and has helped to support the steady expansion of international trade since the 1950s. It is a unique organization in providing a framework for member states to make binding policy commitments that are enforced through a unique dispute settlement system and a variety of transparency mechanisms.

Despite – or because of – its success, the WTO has recently become the focus of vociferous protests by anti-globalization activists. This book separates the facts from the propaganda and provides an accessible overview of the WTO's history, structure, and policies as well as a discussion of the future of the organization. It also confronts the criticisms of the WTO and assesses their validity.

This is essential reading for students of international trade, international political economy, commercial law, and international organizations as well as activists and others interested in a balanced account of a key global institution.

Bernard M. Hoekman is Research Manager of the International Trade team in the Development Research Group of the World Bank, Washington DC, USA.

Petros C. Mavroidis is Edwin B. Parker Professor of Foreign and Comparative Law at Columbia University, USA and Professor of Law at the University of Neuchâtel, Switzerland.

Routledge Global Institutions

Edited by Thomas G. Weiss
The CUNY Graduate Center, New York, USA
and Rorden Wilkinson
University of Manchester, UK

About the Series

The Global Institutions Series is designed to provide readers with comprehensive, accessible, and informative guides to the history, structure, and activities of key international organizations. Every volume stands on its own as a thorough and insightful treatment of a particular topic, but the series as a whole contributes to a coherent and complementary portrait of the phenomenon of global institutions at the dawn of the millennium.

Books are written by recognized experts, conform to a similar structure, and cover a range of themes and debates common to the series. These areas of shared concern include the general purpose and rationale for organizations, developments over time, membership, structure, decision-making procedures, and key functions. Moreover, current debates are placed in historical perspective alongside informed analysis and critique. Each book also contains an annotated bibliography and guide to electronic information as well as any annexes appropriate to the subject matter at hand.

The volumes currently published or under contract include:

The United Nations and Human Rights (2005)
A guide for a new era
by Julie Mertus (American University)

The UN Secretary General and Secretariat (2005)
by Leon Gordenker (Princeton University)

United Nations Global Conferences (2005)
by Michael G. Schechter (Michigan State University)

The UN General Assembly (2005)
by M.J. Peterson (University of Massachusetts, Amherst)

Internal Displacement (2006)
Conceptualization and its consequences
by Thomas G. Weiss (The CUNY Graduate Center) and David A. Korn

Global Environmental Institutions (2006)
by Elizabeth R. DeSombre (Wellesley College)

The International Labour Organization
by Steve Hughes (University of Newcastle)

The Commonwealth(s) and Global Governance
by Timothy Shaw (Royal Roads University)

UNHCR
The politics and practice of refugee protection into the twenty-first century
by Gil Loescher (University of Oxford), James Milner (University of Oxford), and Alexander Betts (University of Oxford)

The International Organization for Standardization and the Global Economy
Setting standards
by Craig Murphy (Wellesley College) and JoAnne Yates (Massachusetts Institute of Technology)

The International Olympic Committee
by Jean-Loup Chappelet (IDHEAP Swiss Graduate School of Public Administration) and Brenda Kübler-Mabbott

The European Union
by Clive Archer (Manchester Metropolitan University)

The World Health Organization
by Kelley Lee (London School of Hygiene and Tropical Medicine)

Internet Governance
The new frontier of global institutions
by John Mathiason (Syracuse University)

Shaping the Humanitarian World
by Peter Walker (Tufts University)

Contemporary Human Rights Ideas
by Bertrand G. Ramcharan (Geneva Graduate Institute of International Studies)

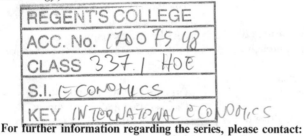
For further information regarding the series, please contact:

Craig Fowlie, Publisher, Politics & International Studies
Taylor & Francis
2 Park Square, Milton Park, Abingdon
Oxford OX14 4RN, UK

+44 (0)207 842 2057 Tel
+44 (0)207 842 2302 Fax

Craig.Fowlie@tandf.co.uk
www.routledge.com

The World Trade Organization

Law, economics, and politics

**Bernard M. Hoekman
and Petros C. Mavroidis**

Routledge
Taylor & Francis Group

LONDON AND NEW YORK

First published 2007
by Routledge
2 Park Square, Milton Park, Abingdon, Oxon OX14 4RN

Simultaneously published in the USA and Canada
by Routledge
270 Madison Ave, New York, NY 10016

Routledge is an imprint of the Taylor & Francis Group, an informa business

© 2007 Bernard M. Hoekman and Petros C. Mavroidis

Typeset in Times New Roman and Helvetica by
Taylor & Francis Books
Printed and bound in Great Britain by
MPG Books Ltd, Bodmin

British Library Cataloguing in Publication Data
A catalogue record for this book is available from the British Library

Library of Congress Cataloging in Publication Data
Hoekman, Bernard M., 1959–
  The World Trade Organization : law, economics and polity /
Bernard M. Hoekman and Petros C. Mavroidis.
    p. cm. – (Routledge global institutions 16)
  Includes bibliographical references and index.
  1. World Trade Organization. 2. Foreign trade regulation.
  3. International trade. I. Mavroidis, Petros C. II. Title.
K4610.H64 2007
382'.92–dc22   2006102047

ISBN 978–0–415–41458–6 (hbk)
ISBN 978–0–415–41459–3 (pbk)
ISBN 978–0–203–94653–7 (ebk)

Contents

Illustrations

Foreword

The current volume is the sixteenth in a dynamic series on "global institutions." The series strives (and, based on the volumes published to date, succeeds) to provide readers with definitive guides to the most visible aspects of what we know as "global governance." Remarkable as it may seem, there exist relatively few books that offer in-depth treatments of prominent global bodies and processes, much less an entire series of concise and complementary volumes. Those that do exist are either out of date, inaccessible to the non-specialist reader, or seek to develop a specialized understanding of particular aspects of an institution or process rather than offer an overall account of its functioning. Similarly, existing books have often been written in highly technical language or have been crafted "in-house" and are notoriously self-serving and narrow.

The advent of electronic media has helped by making information, documents, and resolutions of international organizations more widely available, but it has also complicated matters. The growing reliance on the Internet and other electronic methods of finding information about key international organizations and processes has served, ironically, to limit the educational materials to which most readers have ready access – namely, books. Public relations documents, raw data, and loosely refereed web sites do not make for intelligent analysis. Official publications compete with a vast amount of electronically available information, much of which is suspect because of its ideological or self-promoting slant. Paradoxically, a growing range of purportedly independent web sites offering analyses of the activities of particular organizations has emerged, but one inadvertent consequence has been to frustrate access to basic, authoritative, critical, and well-researched texts. The market for such has actually been reduced by the ready availability of varying quality electronic materials.

For those of us who teach, research, and practice in the area, this access to information has been particularly frustrating. We were delighted, then, when Routledge saw the value of a series that bucks this trend and provides key reference points to the most significant global institutions. They are betting that serious students and professionals will want serious analyses. We have assembled a first-rate line-up of authors to address that market. Our intention, then, is to provide one-stop shopping for all readers – students (both undergraduate and postgraduate), interested negotiators, diplomats, practitioners from nongovernmental and intergovernmental organizations, and interested parties alike – seeking information about the most prominent institutional aspects of global governance.

The World Trade Organization

The World Trade Organization (WTO) needs little introduction. Few global institutions have attracted the kind of public attention it has, let alone in such a short space of time. The mass demonstrations during the organization's Seattle ministerial meeting in late 1999 and again in Cancún four years later (which, though causing less disruption to the meeting, took a macabre turn with the suicide of Korean protestor Lee Kyang Hae) have contributed to a folklore that has grown up around this institution. While other global and regional organizations have certainly had their fair share of displays of public disaffection, they pale in comparison with the theater that routinely accompanies WTO ministerial meetings.

Public interest in the WTO emerged as a consequence of increasing anxiety about the social and political consequences of economic liberalization. Many worried that the competitive pressures to which producers would be exposed as a result of WTO-negotiated market openings would place an increasing strain on already vulnerable workers and a global environment exhibiting numerous signs of distress. Moreover, concerns were raised that the benefits to be had from further liberalization would disproportionately accrue to a small elite of large corporations in the leading industrialized states and not to the large mass of the world's population.[1]

Public interest in the WTO has, however, come with a cost. Although the institution is among the most familiar (often impressively so) of global institutions, many misconceptions prevail. The WTO is a member-driven institution. While the Secretariat is perhaps able to exercise influence at the margins, it does not decide the content of trade negotiations, nor does it decide how negotiations are conducted. Member states, as in all intergovernmental bodies, call the shots. And the manner in which trade negotiations are conducted has evolved from practices first put into place by the original signatories to the General Agreement on Tariffs and Trade (GATT).[2] That said, the degree to which member states are able to exercise influence in content and conduct of negotiations varies greatly and some of the WTO's decision-making procedures are at best described as idiosyncratic.[3]

The profile along with the controversy surrounding and impact of the WTO meant that a book on it was at the top of our list of desirable titles when we first conceived the series in 2004. And next to that entry on our list were the people we most wanted to write the book for us. We were delighted then when Bernard Hoekman and Petros Mavroidis agreed to our initial approach.

They need little introduction. Both are excellent scholars and authorities in their field. Bernard Hoekman is a highly regarded economist and long-standing observer of, as well as participant in, the GATT/ WTO system. He is currently research manager of the international trade team at the World Bank and a research fellow at the Center for Economic Policy Research, and former economist at the GATT. He is co-author of one of the earliest, best-selling, and most widely cited books on the WTO (*The Political Economy of the World Trading System*)[4] and has written more than 150 articles and book chapters on issues relating to trade and development. Petros Mavroidis is a first-rate trade lawyer and renowned authority on the WTO. He is currently Edwin B. Parker Professor of Foreign and Comparative Law at the University of Columbia Law School and Professor of Law at the University of Neuchâtel. He has written 5 books and edited 11 more on international trade and related law as well as published over 70 articles and book chapters.

Hoekman's and Mavroidis' expertise are visible on every page. This book is an authoritative guide to the WTO. Its subtitle – *Law, Economics, and Politics* – indicates the scope of their analysis. It deals in admirable detail with the workings of the institution, the intricacies of the legal agreements that the WTO administers, and considers the future of the organization and the multilateral trading system amid the turbulence of the current round of negotiations. It is an outstanding volume on this most important of institutions. It deserves to be read by all interested in trade, development, governance, and the global economy. As always, comments and suggestions from readers are welcome.

Thomas G. Weiss, The CUNY Graduate Center, New York, USA
Rorden Wilkinson, University of Manchester, UK
March 2007

Acknowledgments

We would like to thank the Editors, Chad Bown, Kyle Bagwell, Jorge Huerta Goldman, Henrik Horn, Rob Howse, Juan-Alberto Marchetti, Aaditya Mattoo, Patrick Messerlin, Marcelo Olarreaga, Caglar Özden, Sheila Page, Susan Prowse, Kamal Saggi, Sergios Stamnas, Alan Sykes, Hannu Wager, Jayashree Watal, Jasper-Martijn Wauters, Alan Winters, and especially Anastasios Tomazos, for comments and helpful discussions on the many subjects that are discussed in this book. We are particularly grateful to Julie Pain and Rhian-Mary Wood-Richards, who assisted us in collection of information and the preparation of the manuscript.

Some of the material in this volume was prepared as part of the project Global Financial and Trade Architecture, supported by the UK Department for International Development.

The views expressed in this book are those of the authors alone and should not be attributed to the World Bank.

Abbreviations

AB	Appellate Body
ACP	African, Caribbean and Pacific
AD	antidumping
CPC	Central Product Classification
CRTA	Committee on Regional Trade Agreements
CTD	Committee on Trade and Development
CVD	countervailing duty
DDAGTF	Doha Development Agenda Trust Fund
DSB	Dispute Settlement Body
DSU	Dispute Settlement Understanding
EC	European Communities
EU	European Union
GATS	General Agreement on Trade in Services
GATT	General Agreement on Tariffs and Trade
GPA	Government Procurement Agreement
GSP	Generalized System of Preferences
HS	Harmonized Commodity Description and Coding System
IMF	International Monetary Fund
INR	initial negotiating right
IPR	intellectual property right
ITA	Information Technology Agreement
ITC	International Trade Centre, Geneva
ITO	International Trade Organization
ITTC	Institute for Training and Technical Cooperation
LDC	least-developed country
MAI	Multilateral Agreement on Investment
MFA	Multifibre Arrangement
MFN	most-favored-nation
NGO	nongovernmental organization

NT	national treatment
NTB	nontariff barrier
OECD	Organization for Economic Cooperation and Development
PRC	People's Republic of China
PTA	preferential trade agreement
QR	quantitative restriction
RPT	reasonable period of time
SCM	subsidies and countervailing measures
SDT	special and differential treatment
SGA	Safeguards Agreement
SPS	Agreement on Sanitary and Phytosanitary Measures
TA	technical assistance
TBT	technical barrier to trade
TNC	Trade Negotiating Committee
TPRM	Trade Policies Review Mechanism
TRIPs	trade-related intellectual property rights
TRQ	tariff rate quota
UN	United Nations
UNCITRAL	United Nations Committee on International Trade Law
UNCTAD	United Nations Conference on Trade and Development
VER	voluntary export restraint
WCO	World Customs Organization
WTO	World Trade Organization

Introduction

Established in 1995, the World Trade Organization (WTO) administers the trade agreements negotiated by its Members, in particular the General Agreement on Tariffs and Trade (GATT), the General Agreement on Trade in Services (GATS), and the Agreement on Trade-related Intellectual Property Rights (TRIPS). The underlying philosophy of the WTO is that open markets and nondiscrimination are conducive to the national welfare of all countries. The *raison d'être* of the WTO is to offer a mechanism to governments to reduce both their own trade barriers and those in foreign markets. Its primary functions are to be a focal point for the negotiation of binding agreements to reduce trade barriers and agree on disciplines for policies affecting international trade, and to provide a mechanism through which WTO Members can enforce these negotiated commitments.

The organization is a stand-alone international institution. It is independent of the United Nations system (that is, it is not a UN specialized agency), in contrast to many other specialized international organizations such as WIPO, ITU, and UNCTAD. The WTO is the successor to the GATT, which it now subsumes. The GATT was never a *formal* international organization; it was an international treaty to which countries and independent customs territories could become a contracting party. The WTO is located on the shore of Lake Geneva in a beautifully landscaped park. Its tranquil environment belies the turbulence that characterized the first ten years of its operation. Few of the officials who were present at the 1994 Ministerial meeting that concluded the Uruguay Round and created the WTO are likely to have foreseen how much controversy the organization would create among nongovernmental organizations (NGOs), parliaments, and industry, farm and labor groups around the world. The WTO has become the focal point of many of those opposing the process of globalization of the world economy.

The visibility of the WTO rose significantly following its 1999 Ministerial meeting in Seattle, USA. Intended to launch a new multilateral round of trade negotiations, the meeting collapsed. A contributory factor to the failure of the meeting was large-scale demonstrations by labor unions, environmental groups and other NGOs, who either supported or opposed specific proposals for expansion of the WTO. Union representatives, for example, were in favor of introducing disciplines on labor standards into the WTO – so as to be able to use the WTO dispute settlement mechanism and the threat of trade sanctions to enforce norms in this area. Many developing countries opposed this, fearing that the real objective of proponents was not to improve working conditions in their countries but to increase their costs of production so as to make their goods less competitive in OECD markets. They also argued that linking trade to labor standards was inappropriate, as trade sanctions would only make working conditions worse in poor countries. A statement by President Clinton at the meeting that he supported discussions on labor standards helped inflame the debate and crystallize developing country opposition to this.

Other contentious issues included suggestions to include disciplines on competition and investment policies in the WTO. The latter had been on the agenda of the OECD for some time, with the objective of negotiating a Multilateral Agreement on Investment (MAI). The draft texts of a MAI that had been proposed by some OECD members had generated great concern among many NGOs – in particular, provisions to allow for so-called investor-state dispute settlement. This would give foreign investors the right to sue host country governments for losses incurred as the result of actions that violated the provisions of the agreement, including changes in policies that would impose additional costs on investors (so-called regulatory takings in US legal parlance). NGOs argued that the MAI was all about defining and strengthening the rights of investors, while not establishing any obligations for them. The extent of opposition to the MAI was strong enough for negotiations to break down in 1998. This reflected not just NGO opposition, but a lack of support by the business community, which concluded that there were so many exceptions being introduced into the text (mostly reflecting national sensitivities regarding specific industries) that it was not worth pushing for. The perception that a significant portion of the MAI agenda would be transferred to the WTO was opposed by many groups in Seattle, as well as by many developing countries that felt that capital-exporting nations would be imposing their preferred investment regimes.

Policies pertaining to labor standards, the environment, or investment involve domestic regulatory instruments. They affect trade, but their primary purpose is to achieve non-trade objectives: guaranteeing specific worker rights; internalizing environmental spillovers; and defining rights and obligations of investors. How governments decide to regulate in such areas will generally vary, reflecting social preferences, physical conditions, and so forth. While regulation may affect foreign firms negatively, that is not necessarily a good reason for seeking to constrain the ability of governments to intervene. However, that is the core traditional function of the WTO: it is an instrument through which governments negotiate agreements that aim to reduce the negative spill-over effects of foreign policies. In the case of its bread and butter, core agenda (trade policies – tariffs, quotas), this does not give rise to the same type of concerns that arise in case of regulatory policies. Any agreements to lower trade barriers will be beneficial for the world as a whole. Some groups that benefited from the protection will be hurt, but overall the aggregate gains from liberalization outweigh the costs. In principle, therefore, there is a surplus that can be used to compensate those who lose if society (government) decides to do so. In practice, this is often not done, helping to explain why trade protection is persistent, but that is another matter. In the case of regulatory policies, it makes no sense to change existing norms if these are considered to be appropriate by a society – they have been put in place to achieve a specific objective. Thus, addressing the international externalities that are created by regulatory standards – or the absence of such regulation – is a much more difficult task than reciprocally bargaining down trade barriers.

Determining where international cooperation on regulatory norms is beneficial for all Members is one of the major challenges confronting the WTO. The active participation of civil society groups in the debates that inform such determinations is a positive development. For the WTO to function effectively it must have the support of Members, which in turn requires that there are (large) constituencies in these member states that regard the rules of the game as being beneficial to them. The more the WTO is pushed by its Members to discipline regulatory policies, the greater the number of stakeholders that will need to be involved in both negotiating and implementing agreements. That in turn has implications for the governance of the WTO.

The WTO is an inter-governmental organization: only governments have legal standing in the organization. GATT practice used to be that deliberations were confidential – little effort was made at what is now called outreach. That has changed in recent years. Information on what is happening and what issues are on the negotiating table is now much easier to obtain, and the extent of interaction between WTO Members, the Secretariat and interested civil society groups has increased. A number of the latter have established offices in Geneva, some of which are larger than those maintained by developing countries – a number of which cannot afford to be present in Geneva at all. However, NGOs or business groups do not have access to WTO deliberations.

The WTO as an organization is quite small and has very few powers. The Secretariat spans some 600 staff (professional and auxiliary), many of whom are translators and secretaries. It has limited responsibilities – essentially to manage meetings and prepare documentation at the request of Members, support dispute settlement proceedings and undertake periodic reviews of the trade policies of Members. Although the head of the organization has tended to be drawn from the ranks of senior political figures from member states (Renato Ruggiero, a former trade minister from Italy; Michael Moore, former Prime Minister of New Zealand; Supachai Panitchpakdi, former Trade and Deputy Prime Minister of Thailand, and at the time of writing Pascal Lamy, former Commissioner for Trade for the European Community) – in contrast to the GATT where the Director-General was generally a senior civil servant – all quickly were made to realize that they had precious little formal authority to take or enforce decisions.[1] As is often stressed by Members, the WTO is a *member-driven organization*, where each signatory has a voice. Even the smallest player can make its voice heard because decision-making is mostly on the basis of consensus. Thus, small countries can, and do, express their views and may block proposals that they do not support. Moreover, because the WTO is a rules-based system where disciplines are enforceable through an effective dispute settlement mechanism, the smallest Member may take on the most powerful country in the world. If a WTO panel decides that the US or the EU has violated a commitment, these large players must bring their measures into compliance with its obligations. The experience suggests that in the majority of cases they do so.[2]

Of course, the rules of the game do reflect power relationships: Uganda does not have the same ability as the United States to determine the outcome of negotiations. Interests differ enormously across WTO Members. Within member states, different constituencies have very different interests as well. While there is nothing new about this, what changed with the establishment of the WTO was that the trading system moved away from a regime where implementation of many rules was voluntary and dispute resolution relied heavily on diplomacy and "pragmatic flexibility," towards one where all rules applied to all Members equally and dispute settlement is more legalistic and "binding."[3] This, in conjunction with a major expansion in the substantive coverage of multilateral disciplines – to also span intellectual property rights and trade in services – and efforts by interest groups of varying stripes to extend its reach further helps explain why the WTO became a focal point for controversy.

Another factor that has played an important role has been the much greater engagement and participation of developing countries in the WTO process. Although press attention tends to center on NGOs, in reality, the failure of the Seattle (1999) and Cancún (2003) ministerial meetings reflected the unwillingness of developing countries to accept the agenda being pushed by certain OECD countries and parts of the NGO community. Thus, Seattle failed in part because of refusal by developing countries to consider the introduction of labor standards in the WTO – strongly supported by many NGOs, often on the basis that this would support development. The Cancún ministerial, a mid-term review meeting of the ongoing Doha Round of negotiations (launched in Doha in 2001), failed because many of the poorest developing countries refused to accept the launch of negotiations on the so-called *Singapore issues* – competition and investment policy, transparency in government procurement and trade facilitation. Although it was later agreed to remove the first three of these subjects from the table, no progress proved possible in key areas such as agriculture, leading to the suspension of the Doha talks in mid-2006. The difficulty in agreeing on negotiating modalities and the agenda of cooperation raises questions about the "design" or "architecture" of the trading system. We return to this question in the final chapter.

To understand what the WTO does, it is necessary to delve into its rules (the law), as well as its operating mechanisms and procedures. For any state or customs territory, WTO membership implies accepting limitations on regulatory autonomy in five areas: (1) trade in goods; (2) trade in services; (3) the protection of intellectual property rights; (4) the settlement of disputes; and (5) periodic review of national trade policies. In what follows, we discuss each of these areas. Our intention is to provide a succinct introduction to the "basics" of the WTO. We start with a brief history of the organization (Chapter 1) and summarize the "nuts and bolts" of how the WTO functions (Chapter 2). Chapters 3 and 4 summarize and explain the rules pertaining to trade in goods, trade in services, and the protection of intellectual property, respectively. Chapter 5 turns to the dispute settlement mechanism, a unique feature of the institution and briefly discusses the procedures in the WTO that aim to increase transparency of Members' trade policies and the so-called plurilateral agreements, of which membership is voluntary. Such agreements may become more prevalent in the future as they are a potential vehicle for subsets of countries to cooperate on issues where no consensus obtains. Chapter 6 focuses on the approach that the GATT/WTO has taken towards addressing the interests of developing countries. The volume concludes in Chapter 7 with a more forward-looking, policy-oriented discussion of the current debates surrounding the functioning and evolution of the WTO, and the directions that the organization may take in the coming years.

We have made significant use of the relevant case law that has developed over time to interpret WTO provisions. We hope the selective citation of the reasoning of dispute settlement panels and the Appellate Body will both help in understanding the core disciplines of the WTO and give a sense of the way the institution operates in practice. While making liberal use of panel and Appellate Body reports as well as some of the WTO legal texts, we have deliberately sought to minimize references to the voluminous literature on the trading system, whether legal or economic. A short select bibliography provides a guide to further reading of other works on the WTO for interested readers.

1 A brief history of the world trading system

The genesis of the GATT in 1947 was the inter-war experience of beggar thy neighbor protectionism, competitive devaluation, and capital controls.[1] Following the adoption of the so-called *Smoot-Hawley Tariff Act*, which raised average US tariffs from 38 to 52 percent, US trading partners imposed retaliatory trade restrictions. A domino effect resulted, as trade flows were diverted to other markets, protectionist measures were taken there, and further retaliation ensued. Once the Second World War was over – indeed, before it was concluded – political leaders sought to establish international institutions to reduce the probability of a repeat performance. New international bodies were designed to manage international relations and monetary and exchange rates (the UN and the IMF) and to assist in financing reconstruction and promoting economic development (the World Bank). An international organization was also foreseen to manage trade relations, the International Trade Organization (ITO). Greater trade was expected to support an increase in real incomes, and non-discriminatory access to markets was expected to reduce the scope for political conflicts or trade disputes spilling over into other domains.

The ITO was supposed to be the institutional framework to administer a set of legal documents referred to as the Havana Charter (HC), after the location where the final negotiation of the so-called Preparatory Committee was held in 1948. The ITO Charter regulated trade in goods and commodity agreements, as well as subjects such as employment policy and restrictive business practices. At the same time, at Lake Success, New York, in early 1947, negotiations between 23 countries – 12 developed and 11 developing – were concluded on the General Agreement on Tariffs and Trade (GATT).[2] Between April and October 1947, the members of the Preparatory Committee conducted a round of tariff negotiations in the course of the ITO negotiations at the European office of the United Nations, in Geneva. This was the first round of multilateral trade negotiations.

The GATT entered into force on 1 January 1948, on a provisional basis, pending the conclusion and the entry into force of the Havana Charter. However, since the Havana Charter never came into force, for its entire 47 years the GATT applied on a "provisional" basis. Following the unwillingness of the US Congress to ratify the ITO Charter (6 December 1950), the GATT slowly developed into an institution of its own, despite the fact that its provisions do not refer to a specific institutional umbrella, as that function was supposed to be played by the ITO. Formally just an international agreement to liberalize trade in goods, *de facto* the GATT gradually evolved into an international institution. A consequence of the lack of institutional foundations was that GATT contracting parties operated on an *ad hoc* basis, with institutional innovations responding to observed needs. This "functional institutionalism" helped to ensure legitimacy because the edifice was built on generally agreed needs. The fact that all decisions were taken by consensus bolstered legitimacy further (consensus implied decisions were adopted as long as no party explicitly opposed them). Thus, while participants in the GATT were formally contracting parties to a treaty,[3] they behaved as members operating under a sketchy "institutional" umbrella.

Accessions to and withdrawals from the GATT/WTO

Accession to the GATT was open to sovereign states and customs territories that possessed full sovereignty over international trade. The latter permitted Hong Kong, China, to become a contracting party to the GATT, and to accede to the WTO. As of 1994, there were 128 GATT contracting parties; this had expanded to 150 WTO Members at the time of writing (Table 1.1).

In order to facilitate accession to the GATT, Art. XXXV GATT allowed for the possibility that acceding countries *not* enter into contractual arrangements *at all* with some incumbent GATT contracting parties. That is, two countries could both be a GATT contracting party, without, however, being bound by the GATT at all in their bilateral relations. The WTO Agreement contains a more detailed version of this institutional possibility (Art. XIII), which states that WTO disciplines shall not apply as between any Member and any other Member if, at the time either becomes a Member, the other does not consent to such application. This non-application clause is not a reservation to the WTO treaty as no reservations to the WTO Agreement

Table 1.1 GATT/WTO negotiating rounds and membership

Name of the round	Chronology	Number of participants
Geneva	1947	19
Annécy	1949	27
Torquay	1950	33
Geneva	1956	36
Dillon	1960–61	43
Kennedy	1962–67	74
Tokyo	1973–79	85
Uruguay	1986–94	128
Doha	2001–	150

are allowed. The non-application provision essentially allows two countries to claim WTO membership while not having any WTO-covered contractual arrangement between each other. At the entry into force of the WTO (1995), seven reservations were made: five by the US against Armenia, Moldova, Georgia, Kyrgyz Republic and Mongolia; one by Turkey against Armenia, and one by El Salvador against China. Most of these were subsequently revoked.

Withdrawal from the GATT was possible under Art. XXXI. For example, after its break from the People's Republic of China (PRC), an original contracting party to the GATT (21 May 1948), the Republic of China, through a letter addressed to the GATT on 5 May 1950, formally withdrew from the GATT.[4]

GATT rounds of trade liberalization

Over time, more countries acceded to the GATT, and the coverage of the treaty expanded and modified. Some major milestones are noted in Table 1.2. The early years involved accession negotiations, a Review Session in the mid-1950s that led to modifications to the treaty, hollowing out of agricultural policy disciplines to reflect US interests, the creation of the European Economic Community (EEC) in 1957, and the introduction of new provisions relating to economic development of poor countries. In 1962, derogations from the GATT rules in the area of trade in cotton textiles were negotiated. These developed into successive multi-year Multifibre Arrangements (MFA-I through MFA-IV) – a complex system of quantitative restrictions that were inconsistent with the basic principles of the GATT.

Starting in the mid-1960s, recurring negotiating rounds expanded the scope of the GATT to cover more nontariff policies. During the

Table 1.2 From GATT to WTO: a chronology

Date	Event
1947	Tariff negotiations between 23 founding parties to the GATT concluded.
1948	GATT provisionally enters into force on 1 January 1948. Delegations from 53 countries sign the so-called Havana Charter establishing an ITO in March 1948.
1949	Annécy Round of tariff negotiations.
1950	China withdraws from GATT. The US Administration abandons efforts to seek Congressional ratification of the ITO.
1951	Torquay Round of tariff negotiations. Germany (Federal Republic) accedes.
1955	A review session modifies numerous provisions of the GATT. The US is granted a waiver from GATT disciplines for certain agricultural policies. Japan accedes to the GATT.
1956	Fourth round of multilateral negotiations is held in Geneva.
1960	A council of representatives is created to manage day-to-day activities. The Dillon Round is launched.
1961	Dillon Round concluded. The "Short-Term Arrangement" permitting quota restrictions on exports of cotton textiles agreed as an exception to GATT rules.
1962	The Short-Term becomes the Long-Term Arrangement on Cotton Textiles.
1964	The Kennedy Round begins.
1965	Part IV (on Trade and Development) is added to the GATT, establishing new guidelines for trade policies of – and towards – developing countries. A Committee on Trade and Development is created to monitor implementation.
1967	Kennedy Round concludes.
1973	The Tokyo Round starts.
1974	The Agreement Regarding International Trade in Textiles, better known as the Multifibre Arrangement (MFA) enters into force, replacing the Long-Term Agreement. The MFA restricts export growth to 6 percent per year.
1979	Tokyo Round concludes. Includes a set of "codes of conduct" on a variety of trade policy areas that countries can decide to sign on a voluntary basis. Most codes predominantly attract OECD membership.
1982	A GATT Ministerial meeting – the first in almost a decade – fails to agree on an agenda for a new round.
1986	After lengthy preparatory work, including national studies on trade in services, the Uruguay Round is launched in Punta del Este, Uruguay.
1990	A Ministerial meeting in Brussels fails to conclude the Uruguay Round.

1993	Three years after the scheduled end of negotiations, the Uruguay Round is concluded on 15 December on the basis of a "Single Undertaking" – virtually all negotiated disciplines apply to all countries, albeit with differing transition periods and subject to special provisions for developing countries. Agreements include new rules for trade in services, intellectual property rights, and a stronger dispute settlement mechanism.
1994	At an April Ministerial in Marrakech, the Final Act establishing the WTO and embodying the results of the Uruguay Round is accepted.
1995	The WTO enters into force on 1 January.
1996	Maritime services talks collapse. The first WTO Ministerial conference hosted by Singapore, creates working groups on trade and investment, trade and competition policy, transparency in public procurement and trade facilitation.
1997	Forty governments agree to eliminate tariffs on computer and telecommunication products by the year 2000 (the Information Technology Agreement). Negotiations on an Agreement on Basic Telecommunications and a Financial Services Agreement are concluded under GATS auspices.
1999	Ministerial meeting in Seattle fails to launch a new "Millennium" round.
2001	A new round is launched in Doha, Qatar, the Doha Development Agenda, spanning trade in agriculture, manufactures, and services. Agreement to launch negotiations on the four Singapore issues if "explicit consensus" to do so exists at the next Ministerial meeting in 2003.
2002	EU launches negotiations with African, Caribbean and Pacific states to convert unilateral trade preference regimes into reciprocal free trade agreements – Economic Partnership Agreements.
2003	The "mid-term" review Ministerial meeting in Cancún collapses amid disagreement on whether to launch negotiations on the four so-called Singapore issues, as well as differences on agriculture, including the treatment of cotton subsidies, and special and differential treatment of developing countries.
2004	In July, a negotiating framework is agreed and removes three of the four Singapore issues – leaving only one (trade facilitation), paving the way for continued negotiations. Ten new countries accede to the EU, bringing total membership to 25.
2005	The final stage of the Agreement on Textiles and Clothing is implemented, abolishing remaining quantitative restrictions on imports imposed by WTO members.
2006	The Doha Round is declared to be in a state of suspension. The US signs its 15th bilateral trade agreement. The number of preferential trade agreements notified to the WTO passes 250.

Source: Adapted from Bernard M. Hoekman and Michel M. Kostecki, *The Political Economy of the World Trading System* (Oxford: Oxford University Press, 2001); updated and expanded by the authors.

GATT years, the Contracting Parties conducted eight rounds of multilateral negotiations (Table 1.2). Up to the Kennedy Round, negotiators were essentially preoccupied with the reduction of tariff barriers. However, the Kennedy Round shifted the focus of the negotiations to nontariff barriers (NTBs), which had begun to be viewed as a formidable obstacle to trade liberalization. Negotiators had originally understood the term NTBs to refer to nontariff barriers imposed for economic reasons (antidumping, countervailing, safeguards).

Over time, first through the negotiation of the Agreement on Technical Barriers to Trade (TBT) in the Tokyo Round and then through the re-negotiation of this agreement and negotiation of the Agreement on Sanitary and Phytosanitary Measures (SPS) during the Uruguay Round, trading partners began to negotiate on nontariff policies that were unconnected, in principle at least, to the competitive position of domestic industries. In the Uruguay Round, disciplines on intellectual property rights and trade in services were negotiated. Thus, the trading system was extended to cover a number of domestic policies affecting industrial structure and regulatory frameworks that were argued by some Members, most notably the United States, to impede "market access" abroad, even if they could not, across the board, plausibly be understood as discriminatory protection of domestic industries.

The evolution of the legal framework of the GATT/WTO has been driven by political bargaining, with the terms of the bargain at any point in time (and changes over time) influenced by both governmental and non-governmental actors. Initially largely a tariff agreement, as average tariffs fell over time, and attention shifted to nontariff policies, the set of interest groups seeking to add agenda items changed. The importance of specific interest groups cannot be overstated. Thus, the extension of the WTO to include agreements on services and trade-related intellectual property rights was driven by a desire on the part of OECD industry groups (telecom providers, banks, pharmaceutical firms) to improve access to foreign markets for their products. The significant deepening of disciplines on policies affecting trade in agricultural products and textiles and clothing was in part the *quid pro quo* demanded by developing countries for this extension. In turn, this *quid pro quo* was needed because in the 1960s and 1970s agriculture and textiles and clothing had to a large extent been removed from the ambit of GATT rules and disciplines – reflecting the power of the workers and farmers employed in these sectors.

Trade tensions and clashes between the Members have often played a role in defining the agenda of negotiations and the evolution of disciplines – in effect identifying where rules were needed or should be clarified. Another driver for new disciplines was the emergence of US unilateralism in the 1980s, as reflected in provisions such as Section 301 of the 1974/1988 US Trade Act, which required the US Trade Representative to identify and potentially retaliate against countries that maintained policies that were detrimental to US exports, including non-protection of US intellectual property. As discussed later in this volume, such pressure was not always successful. Thus, EU insistence on expansion of the WTO to cover investment and competition policies failed during the Doha Round, as have recurrent efforts by some Members to put labor standards on the table.

2 The WTO in a nutshell

As explained above, the GATT lacked an institutional structure – in the early years of its operation it did not even exist as an entity except when formal meetings of the contracting parties were held. It is precisely this gap that the WTO came to fill. However, the WTO did not start from a clean slate. A lot of the institutional design that the GATT put into place through, essentially, "learning by doing," provided inspiration to the architects of the current world trade regime.

The Preamble of the GATT 1947 lists among its objectives raising standards of living, ensuring full employment and a large and steadily growing volume of real income and effective demand, developing the full use of the resources of the world and expanding the production and exchange of goods. It goes on to say that reciprocal and mutually advantageous arrangements involving a substantial reduction of tariffs and other barriers to trade as well as the elimination of discriminatory treatment in international trade will contribute to the realization of these objectives. Nowhere is any mention made of free trade as an ultimate goal. This continues to be the case under the WTO. Thus, contrary to popular belief, the *formal* objective of the WTO is *not* free trade. Trade is a means to achieve the objectives listed in the Preamble, not an end in itself.

The WTO agreement is a *single undertaking* – all its provisions apply to all Members. This is a major difference with the 1947 GATT, where countries could decide whether or not to sign new agreements. Another major difference is in the dispute settlement area. Under the WTO, it is virtually impossible to block the formation of dispute settlement panels, the adoption of panel reports and the authorization to retaliate, whereas this was possible under the GATT. Yet another difference is that the WTO has a stronger mandate to pursue transparency and surveillance functions, in part through the *Trade Policy Review Mechanism.*

Nuts and bolts

In a nutshell, the WTO is both a mechanism for exchanging (trading) trade policy commitments, and agreeing on a code of conduct. The WTO comprises a negotiated set of specific legal obligations that regulate trade policies of member states. These are embodied in the GATT-1994, the GATS, and the TRIPS agreements. The WTO does not define or specify trade outcomes, i.e., it does not seek to manage trade flows. Seven dimensions of the WTO are of particular importance in understanding the operation and function of the institution:

1 single undertaking;
2 tariffs are the only permissible form of protection;
3 non-discrimination;
4 reciprocity;
5 enforcement of obligations;
6 transparency;
7 safety valves.

Single undertaking

There are three layers of legal obligations that can be assumed when adhering to the WTO:

1 an *inflexible, multilateral* set of obligations: provisions that bind all Members upon accession. A country joining the WTO has no option but to abide by this set of obligations,[1] which are reflected in the WTO Agreement itself and all its annexes (the so-called *multilateral* agreements);
2 a *flexible, multilateral* set of obligations: provisions that bind only those WTO Members which have acceded to the corresponding WTO legal instruments. Such obligations exist because the WTO law, besides the *multilateral* agreements, also allows the so-called *plurilateral* agreements, that is, agreements the participation to which is optional;
3 a *bilateral* set of obligations. These are *sui generis* obligations which are assumed by the acceding WTO Member and regulate in a specific manner its legal relations with the incumbent WTO Members. For example, during the negotiations that led to the accession of the People's Republic of China (PRC) to the WTO, a special safeguard was concluded which, contrary to what is required under the

WTO Safeguards Agreement, allows WTO Members to impose discriminatory (i.e., country-specific) safeguards against the PRC.[2]

Protection through tariffs only

The term "protection" does not appear as such in the WTO agreement. It is implicit, however, in the term *non-discrimination*. While there is no operational definition of the term "protection,"[3] in this book, it captures measures that are primarily intended to favor domestic over foreign production.[4] With respect to trade in goods, the only form of permitted protection for domestic products is the tariff. WTO Members cannot use quotas to restrict trade in goods.

Non-discrimination

The principle of non-discrimination has two components, the most-favored nation (MFN) rule and the national treatment (NT) principle. The MFN rule requires that a product made in one Member country be treated no less favorably than a "like" (very similar) product that originates in any other country.[5] National treatment requires that foreign products – once they have satisfied whatever border measures are applied (once they have paid their "ticket to entry" in a particular market) – be treated no less favorably than like or directly competitive domestic products. As discussed below, this applies to both fiscal and other policies (regulations). In both cases, the obligation is to provide foreign products treatment more favourable than that afforded to their domestic counterparts. A government is free to discriminate in favor of foreign products (against domestic goods) if it desires, subject, of course, to the MFN rule – all foreign products must be given the same treatment. While MFN applies unconditionally, exceptions are made for the formation of free trade areas or customs unions, preferential treatment of developing countries, and, as already noted, upon accession of a new Member, an existing Member may invoke the WTO's non-application clause (Article XIII).

MFN has a number of desirable properties, both economic and political.[6] On the economic front, if policy does not discriminate between foreign suppliers, importers and consumers will continue to have an incentive to source from the lowest-cost foreign supplier. In addition to this efficiency argument, non-discrimination is an effective defense against "concession erosion" which could otherwise materialize and give negotiators less incentive to continue liberalizing. That is, absent an MFN-type of discipline, country A might not want to negotiate with country B if it feels that B might later negotiate with country C in a manner that will undercut its promise to A. On the political side, MFN offers smaller countries a guarantee that larger countries will not exploit their market power against them, or give better treatment to competitors for foreign policy reasons. MFN also helps maintain cooperation by raising the costs to a country of defecting from its negotiated commitments. If it desires to raise trade barriers, it must apply these to all WTO Members. This raises the political cost of backsliding, gives greater incentives for domestic pro-trade interests to support negotiations in the WTO and thus enhances the credibility (value) of commitments. Finally, MFN reduces negotiating costs – once a negotiation has been concluded with a country, the results extend to all. This obviates the need for other countries to negotiate similar treatment. Instead, negotiations can be limited to so-called principal suppliers.

The role of national treatment is to ensure that liberalization commitments are not offset through the imposition of domestic taxes and similar measures (it is hence, another dimension of the concession erosion argument, except that this time the erosion benefits domestic products). As discussed below, it is a very wide-ranging rule. The obligation applies whether or not a specific tariff commitment was made, and covers all policies. It is irrelevant whether or to what extent a discriminatory policy hurts an exporter – what matters is the existence of discrimination.

Reciprocity

Reciprocity is a basic principle that applies to negotiations. It is not a legal principle. It is aimed at limiting the scope for free riding that may arise because of the MFN rule and the desire to obtain a *quid pro quo* for own trade liberalization. Generally, nations are quite successful in minimizing free riding. For example, *internalization,* defined as the sum of all imports originating in countries with which a country exchanges concessions as a percentage of total imports of goods on which concessions are made, was about 90 percent for the US in the Dillon (1960–61) and Kennedy (1964–67) Rounds.[7] Reciprocity is often defined in what Jagdish Bhagwati has called "first-difference" terms, and not absolutely. That is, countries seek to make equivalent changes in policies, as opposed to striving to establish equal absolute levels of protection.

Reciprocity applies in a rather specific sense when countries accede to the WTO. Given that new Members obtain all the benefits in terms of market access that have resulted from earlier negotiating rounds, existing Members invariably demand that potential entrants pay an "admission fee." In practice, this implies not only that a country's trade regime conforms to the WTO rules, but that the acceding government liberalizes access to its market as well. Here there is no *quid pro quo* in that the acceding country cannot ask for greater market access in return – what it gets is the sum total of all commitments negotiated among Members in the past.

The rationale for reciprocity can be found in the political economy literature. Costs of liberalization generally are concentrated in specific industries, which often will be well organized and oppose reductions in protection. Benefits, while in the aggregate usually greater than costs, accrue to a much larger set of agents, who thus do not have a great individual incentive to organize themselves politically. By obtaining a reduction in foreign import barriers as a *quid pro quo* for a reduction in domestic trade restrictions, specific export-oriented domestic interests that will gain from liberalization have an incentive to support it in domestic political markets. For reciprocity to work it is important that lobbies favoring open markets do not have other means of getting what they want. One such alternative is to negotiate increased market access on a bilateral basis. Such bilateral alternatives weaken the power of reciprocity in the multilateral context, as they reduce the incentives for export interests to support multilateral liberalization.

Enforcement of obligations

If a country perceives that actions taken by another government have the effect of nullifying or impairing negotiated market access commitments or the disciplines of the WTO, it may bring this to the attention of the government involved and ask that the policy be brought into compliance. If satisfaction is not obtained, it may invoke WTO dispute settlement procedures. These involve the establishment of panels of impartial experts who are charged with determining whether a contested measure violates the WTO. Because the WTO is an inter-governmental agreement, private parties do not have legal standing before the WTO's dispute settlement body. Only governments have the right to bring cases. The existence of dispute settlement procedures precludes the use of unilateral retaliation. This is particularly important for small countries, as unilateral actions will be ineffective and thus not be credible.

Transparency

A pre-condition for enforcement is information on the trade regimes that are maintained by Members. Transparency is a legal obligation, embedded in Article X GATT, Article III GATS and Article 63 TRIPS, and in numerous provisions in agreements on specific trade policy instruments. WTO Members are required to publish their trade regulations, to establish and maintain institutions allowing for the review of administrative decisions affecting trade, to respond to requests for information by other Members, and to notify changes in trade policies to the WTO. There are over 200 notification requirements embodied in the various WTO agreements and decisions. All of these require the existence of appropriate bodies or agencies in Members that have the responsibility of satisfying them. These internal transparency requirements are supplemented by multilateral surveillance of trade policies by WTO Members, facilitated by periodic country-specific reports (Trade Policy Reviews) that are prepared by the Secretariat and discussed in the WTO Council – the so-called Trade Policy Review Mechanism.

Transparency is vital in terms of ensuring "ownership" of the WTO as an institution – if citizens do not know what the organization does, its legitimacy will be eroded. The Trade Policy Reviews are a unique source of information that can be used by civil society to assess what the implications are of the overall trade policies that are pursued by their government. From an economic perspective, transparency can also help reduce trade policy-related uncertainty and thus risk premia that are required by investors.

Safety valves

The WTO recognizes that governments may need flexibility to restrict trade in specific circumstances. Three types of provisions allow for the use of trade measures: to attain non-economic objectives, ensure "fair competition," and intervention in trade for economic reasons. The first include provisions allowing for policies to protect public health or national security, and to protect industries that are seriously injured by competition from imports. The underlying idea in the latter case is generally that governments should have the right to step in when competition seriously injures domestic competitors. Although not explicitly mentioned in the relevant WTO agreement, the underlying rationale for intervention is that such competition causes political and social problems associated with the need for the industry to adjust to changed circumstances. Second, "fair trade" type of measures include the right to impose countervailing duties on imports that have been subsidized and antidumping duties on imports that have been dumped – sold at a price that is below that charged in the home market. Finally, the third type of "safety valve" allows for actions to be taken if there are serious balance-of-payments difficulties, or if a government desires to support an infant industry. In other words, one way to present the GATT is as follows: trading nations exchange promises about *default* tariffs, and about *state contingency* tariffs, the latter corresponding to contingencies ranging from health-related to producer welfare-related concerns.[8]

Structure and operation of the WTO

Four Annexes to the WTO define the substantive rights and obligations of Members. Annex 1 has three parts: comprising the GATT, the GATS; and the Agreement on Trade-Related Aspects of Intellectual Property Rights (TRIPS), respectively. Annex 2 comprises the Understanding on Rules and Procedures Governing the Settlement of Disputes. Annex 3 contains the Trade Policy Review Mechanism (TPRM). Annex 4 covers so-called Plurilateral Trade Agreements that bind only signatories.

The WTO is charged (Art. II) with facilitating the implementation and operation of the Multilateral Trade Agreements (as embodied in Annexes 1–3), providing a forum for negotiations, administering the dispute settlement understanding (DSU), and multilateral surveillance of trade policies. It is also charged with cooperating with the World Bank and the IMF to achieve greater coherence in global economic policy-making (Article III). The WTO is headed by a Ministerial Conference of all Members, meeting at least once every two years. As can be seen from the chronology in Table 1.1, many of these meetings have ended in failure – something to which we return below.

Between meetings of the Ministerial Conference the organization is managed by a General Council at the level of officials – usually ambassadors or senior representatives based in Geneva. The General Council turns itself, as needed, into a body to adjudicate trade disputes (the Dispute Settlement Body – DSB) or to review trade policies of the Member countries (the Trade Policy Review Body). Three subsidiary councils operate under the general guidance of the General Council (Figure 2.1): the Council for Trade in Goods; the Council for Trade in Services; and the Council for Trade-Related Aspects of Intellectual Property Rights. Separate committees deal with the operation of specific agreements or WTO disciplines (e.g., surveillance of regional trade agreements; trade–environment linkages; and the WTO's finances and administration). In addition to these standing bodies, working groups may be established to deal with issues on the

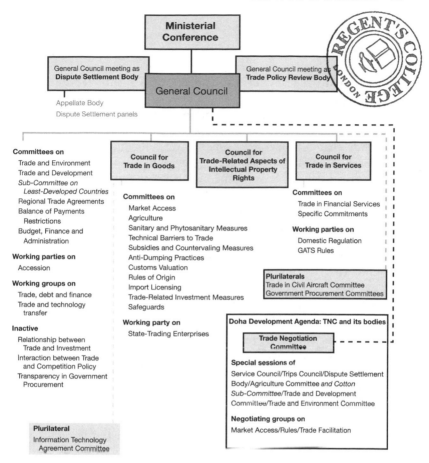

Figure 2.1 The structure of the WTO

basis of terms of reference determined by the WTO Council or a subsidiary body.

All WTO Members may participate in all Councils, committees, and so forth, except dispute settlement panels, the Appellate Body (AB), the Textiles Monitoring Body – created to oversee the implementation of the Agreement on Textiles and Clothing, and committees dealing with plurilateral agreements. Generally only the larger Members regularly participate in most meetings. Poor developing countries often are not represented at WTO meetings. Many have no delegation in Geneva, and those that do invariably are not adequately staffed to allow participation in all meetings.

In total, the various WTO bodies, both standing and *ad hoc*, including working parties on accession (averaging around 25 in the 1995–2006 period), dispute settlement panels, and informal consultations of Members imply there are over 2,000 meetings a year at or around the WTO headquarters in Geneva. As mentioned, the day-to-day activities are undertaken by officials affiliated with a delegation, generally working on the basis of instructions from capitals or by delegations that have come for a specific meeting from the capital. A metaphor that is sometimes used to describe the operation of the WTO is a geographically dispersed network of officials based in Geneva and national capitals, complemented by national business and non-governmental organizations that lobby their governments to defend their interests in the WTO. Only governments have standing in the WTO, however, and only government representatives have access to formal meetings.[9]

The WTO Secretariat is relatively small, and has little independent power.[10] As is often stressed by governments, the WTO is a "Member-driven" organization – the Secretariat is there to assist in the preparation and organization of meetings, as directed by the Chairs of the respective bodies, generally a delegate from a Member who has been appointed by the other Members. The Secretariat has very little scope to take initiatives on its own authority. Thus, decisions to launch dispute settlement actions or negotiations are the sole responsibility of WTO Members, not the Secretariat. It is important to understand the limitations that are imposed on the Secretariat. Critics of "the WTO" often direct their criticism of the workings of the organization at the Secretariat, which has borne the brunt of widespread attacks since the creation of the WTO. Any such criticism should be directed at the membership, not the Secretariat. In contrast to the IMF or the World Bank, where management has considerable latitude to interpret and implement a specific mandate that has been delegated to it, WTO management is subject to close oversight from the WTO membership.[11]

The WTO Secretariat's job is largely to provide Members with technical and logistical support, including organizing meetings of governing bodies and preparing background documentation when requested by committees, working groups or negotiating groups. The support provided by the Secretariat has extended to technical assistance to Members and training activities. The magnitude of such activity expanded significantly after 2000, supported by extra-budgetary resources provided by a subset of the membership in the form of a trust fund. The increased importance given to technical assistance and training activities was also reflected in the creation of a stand-alone institute, the WTO Institute for Training and Technical Cooperation (ITTC). The ITTC administers the WTO's annual technical assistance (TA) plans. Although responsible for policy and coordination of such assistance, delivery is in large part dependent on the operational Divisions of the WTO, which take charge of delivery of training and technical assistance within their respective areas of competence. A significant proportion of WTO staff time is dedicated to participation in workshops and seminars in developing country members.

The increase in training activities is a response to the challenges developing country Members confront in coping with the increasing demands posed by the multilateral trading system. During the Doha Round, Members agreed to create a special *Doha Development Agenda Trust Fund* (DDAGTF) in which all funds for TA would be placed without any earmarking by donors, with the Secretariat reporting to the WTO *Committee on Trade and Development* (CTD). At the time of writing, the DDAGTF had an annual budget of some CHF 25 million, equivalent to some 10 percent of the WTO budget. The budget of the WTO in 2005 was approximately CHF 250 million. Financial contributions to the budget of the WTO are based on each Member's share in total trade, with a minimum contribution for countries with a very small share. The top ten traders account for over two-thirds of total contributions. The EU contribution is assessed separately for each of its member states, and includes intra-EU trade.

Negotiating mechanisms and approaches

It takes a decision by the WTO membership (at Ministerial Conference-level) to launch a round of negotiations. In recent rounds, a Trade Negotiating Committee (TNC) was established to supervise the negotiations. All WTO Members and the Director-General of the WTO participate in the TNC. In the Doha Round (unlike previous rounds), the Ministerial Conference set deadlines to achieve results. Negotiations rarely meet deadlines – they are almost invariably broken. Negotiations are completed successfully only when the entire membership is satisfied with the results. In practice, the only binding deadline has been the expiration of "fast-track" negotiating authority for the US executive, under which Congress agrees to vote on the outcome of negotiations on an up or down basis, without reopening any of the specifics of the package that was negotiated.

Negotiations in the WTO on market access matters can take different forms. So-called request-offer negotiations have been very frequent and continue to be a core mechanism. They involve one member asking another to make a specific concession – reduce a tariff on a certain good or set of goods, limit expenditure on production subsidies, remove barriers to foreign participation in a service market, and so forth – and the other member responding with an offer and a request of its own. This *quid pro quo* bargaining is a central element of negotiations. The MFN rule ensures that all concessions that are eventually agreed are extended to all other Members.

Request-offer negotiations may be supplemented or replaced with formula approaches that revolve around a specific rule that will be applied to reforming a specific policy area. Examples are tariff-cutting formulae under which all tariff bindings will be reduced by 35 percent – a so-called linear cut – or more complex "non-linear" formulae that cut higher tariffs proportionately more than lower tariffs. The best-known example of such a non-linear formula that has been used in negotiations is the "Swiss formula."[12] One effect of such formulae is to reduce the dispersion in the level of tariff bindings of Members.

Formula approaches may also take the form of zero-for-zero negotiations, where the objective is to remove tariffs on a specific set of products or a sector. An example where this occurred is the Information Technology Agreement (ITA), under which signatories agreed to remove tariffs on a set of information technology goods. A challenge in the pursuit of such negotiations is to ensure that enough Members participate to remove concerns about free riding by non-signatories. In the case of the ITA, the agreement stipulated that participants representing approximately 90 percent of world trade would have to notify their acceptance of the ITA by 1 April 1997 for it to enter into force. The original 29 signatories did not reach this 90 percent trade coverage criteria, since they collectively accounted for only 83 percent of world trade in information technology products. However, in the months after the Singapore Ministerial, a number of other countries expressed an interest in becoming participants in the ITA, so that the 90 percent criterion was met, the ITA entered into force, with the first staged reductions in tariffs occurring on 1 July 1997. Following ITA I, an ITA II was successfully concluded. All results of the ITA negotiations were subsequently "multilateralized," and apply on a non-discriminatory basis. Thus, the ITA is not a plurilateral agreement.

In the case of services, negotiations have mostly taken the form of request-offer approaches, although formulae have also been used. In the latter case the focal point has not been on the average level of protection or its dispersion, but on the types of disciplines that

Members would adopt. An example is the so-called Reference paper for Basic Telecommunications, under which Members commit to putting in place independent regulatory bodies and ensuring access to networks for foreign providers on common terms. In the Doha Round, efforts were made by some Members to obtain agreement on so-called model schedules, with provisions that all would agree to commit to. As in the case of the ITA and other zero-for-zero negotiations for trade in goods, in services there have also been concerns about free riding, given that the depth of participation in the GATS is to a large extent a function of the specific commitments made by a Member. In the case of negotiations of financial services, the major players required that a critical mass of countries joined the relevant agreement (see Chapter 4). In the case of both goods (GATT) and services (GATS), the least developed countries can generally free ride, in that they are often not required to make market access liberalizing commitments. While generally defended on "development" grounds, in practice, such free riding is permitted because the countries concerned are so small (poor) that their markets are of little interest to exporters in the rest of the world.

No formal mechanisms exist for civil society groups, including the private sector, to participate in negotiations or the deliberations of standing committees and other WTO bodies. Such groups must instead lobby their governments at home and exert pressure through the media and demonstrations. This is a reflection of the two-level game that characterizes the functioning of the trading system: it is a game where only governments play at the WTO level, but all affected and interested groups determine the stance that these governments take in negotiations. Which of these groups are most influential at the national – or international – level is very much endogenous, and depends on many factors, including the type of government in the various Members. Relative to the GATT period, NGOs have become much more active and influential in the WTO process.

Decision-making

Most decision-making is based on consensus. Consensus does not mean unanimity. It signifies that no delegation represented in a meeting objects to a proposal. Achieving consensus can be a complex process, requiring issue linkages. Consensus reinforces conservative tendencies in the system. Proposals for change can be adopted only if unopposed. Although it creates the potential for paralysis, consensus helps enhance the legitimacy of decisions.

Although, in practice, consensus rules, formally recourse can be made to voting on the basis of "one Member-one vote." Weighted voting – say, on the basis of share in world trade – is not foreseen in the WTO.[13] If voting occurs, unanimity is required for amendments concerning general, core principles such as MFN or national treatment. Interpretation of the provisions of the WTO agreements and decisions on waivers of a Member's obligations require approval by a three-quarters majority vote. A two-thirds majority is needed for amendments relating to issues other than general principles mentioned above. Where not otherwise specified and where consensus cannot be reached, a simple majority vote is in principle sufficient. Art. X WTO specifies that a Member is not bound by any amendment that passes a vote if it is opposed to it, and the change is such as to alter its rights and obligations. The Ministerial Conference may ask a Member that does not accept an amendment to withdraw from the WTO or to grant it a waiver. As the latter makes little sense if it concerns a large country, and small countries are unlikely to be "worth the trouble," this is not something that can be expected to occur. Moreover, it should be noted that legislative amendments in practice are pursued as part of a broader multilateral negotiation. In practice, voting does not occur. WTO Members decided not to apply provisions allowing for a vote in the case of accessions and requests for waivers, but to continue to proceed on the basis of consensus.

Given a membership of 150 converging on a prospective 175+, consensus is feasible to deal with day-to-day issues, many of which will be of interest to only a subset of the membership, but becomes a potential problem if it is used strategically by a Member to achieve things that it wants, or, alternatively, to block progress on an issue. Traditionally, the approach taken to hammer out possible deals on contentious issues is through small group meetings involving principals and interested parties. The term to describe such meetings became the Green room, originally based on the decoration found in a meeting room adjacent to the WTO Director-General's offices where such small group interactions were often held. A convention has since emerged to call such meetings Green room gatherings, no matter where they are held.

The Green room process became very controversial in the late 1990s, as many developing countries (supported by NGOs concerned about transparency and inclusion) objected to being excluded. As discussed in the final chapter of this volume, proposals have been made for several decades now to formalize the Green room process by creating an executive committee to manage the WTO agenda, with a core permanent membership based on agreed criteria such as share in world trade, in addition to a rotating set of smaller Members. To date, no progress in this direction has proven possible in the WTO. The fact is that, given the large membership of the WTO, something analogous to a Green room process is unavoidable. During the Doha Round, efforts were made to make the Green room process more inclusive and transparent. One mechanism that was adopted was to appoint specific Ministers as "facilitators" at Ministerial meetings with the task of consulting and transmitting the substance of discussions on a topic to all Members. The emergence of a greater number of coalitions such as the G-20 group can also be seen as a mechanism to reduce transactions costs.

Although it is often argued by critics that one of the major failings of the WTO is a lack of transparency of its operations, great progress has been made on this front. The WTO Internet home page provides access to most of the documentation that is prepared by and submitted to the WTO – documents that under GATT 1947 procedures were "restricted" and not made available to the public. That said, it continues to be the case that not all of the data generated by the WTO is freely available. Examples include the WTO Integrated Database, which comprises all of the tariff bindings to which Members have committed themselves, the detailed data underlying the TPR reports, and so-called Job serial documents, frequently used in the Doha negotiations to present new ideas or proposals.

3   The GATT

The original GATT contract underwent a substantial transformation during the Uruguay round: WTO Members agreed to *add* to the original text of the GATT a series of Understandings adopted during the Uruguay Round, as well as the so-called GATT *acquis*: the decisions adopted by the GATT CONTRACTING PARTIES since 1947, including protocols of tariff concessions, accessions and waivers still in force.[1] In what follows we discuss the meaning and substance of the main legal disciplines of the GATT – the key Articles are summarized in Box 3.1. Space constraints preclude any in-depth discussion of the underlying economic or policy issues. We will return to some of these in Chapter 7, but in order to understand the substance of the GATT a more "legal" treatment is required.[2]

Box 3.1 Summary of the main GATT Articles

I   MFN requirement.
II   Tariff schedules (bindings).
III   National treatment.
V   Freedom of transit of goods.
VI   Allows antidumping and countervailing duties. Superseded by the GATT 1994 Agreement on Antidumping, and the Agreement on Subsidies and Countervailing Measures (SCM).
VII   Valuation of goods for customs purposes to be based on actual value. Superseded by the GATT 1994 Agreement on the Implementation of Article VII.
VIII   Fees connected with import and export formalities to be cost-based.
X   Obligation to publish trade laws and regulations.
XI   Prohibition on quantitative restrictions.

XII	Permits trade restrictions to safeguard the balance of payments.
XIII	Non-discriminatory administration of quantitative restrictions.
XVI	Prohibits export subsidies. Complemented by the WTO Agreement on Subsidies and Countervailing Measures.
XVII	State trading enterprises to abide by MFN.
XVIII	Allows developing countries to restrict trade to promote infant industries and to protect the balance-of-payments (weaker conditionality than Article XII).
XIX	Allows for emergency action to restrict imports of particular products if these cause serious injury to the domestic industry. Complemented by the WTO Agreement on Safeguards.
XX	General exceptions provision—allows trade restrictions if necessary to attain non-economic objectives (health, safety).
XXI	National security exception.
XXII	Requires consultations between parties involved in trade disputes.
XXIII	GATT's main dispute settlement provision, providing for violation and non-violation complaints. Complemented by the WTO Understanding on Rules and Procedures Governing the Settlement of Disputes.
XXIV	Lays out criteria for the formation of free trade areas and customs unions.
XXVIII	Allows for renegotiation of tariff concessions.
XXVIII *bis*	Calls for periodic trade rounds to lower trade barriers.
XXXIII	Allows for accession of new members.
P IV	Calls for more favorable and differential treatment of developing countries.

Border measures[3]

There are two types of border measures: quantitative restrictions (QRs) and tariffs. WTO membership brings with it the obligation to abolish QRs (Art. XI GATT) and to participate in tariff negotiations (Art. XXVIII *bis*) aimed at establishing tariff ceilings for products. Such negotiated ceilings, generally called tariff "bindings," establish maximum levels that applied tariffs may not exceed.

The cornerstone of the GATT is the principle of non-discrimination. It takes the form of a legal obligation that binds the actions of WTO

Members with respect to both border (trade) policies and internal regulatory or tax policies, i.e., measures destined to apply to both domestic products and imports alike. A comprehensive reading of Arts. I, II, III, XI and XVI GATT and the associated case law implies that since (import and export) quantitative restrictions are prohibited (Art. XI GATT), and subsidies are regulated (Art. XVI GATT and the WTO Agreement on Subsidies and Countervailing Measures, SCM), the only permissible form of protection of domestic products is through customs duties (Art. II GATT).

Customs duties, other border measures and non-discrimination (MFN)

Irrespective of whether duties have been bound or not, they must be applied on a non-discriminatory basis (Art. I). Since customs duties concern only imported products, the legal obligation amounts to a prohibition on discrimination between two imported products. For tariff commitments to be meaningful, a common language to describe goods is required: otherwise it is difficult to make any claim that country A discriminates against cars originating in B by subjecting them to an import regime worse than that afforded to cars originating in C. There is a need to have a *common understanding* as to what a *car*, in this example, amounts to. The Harmonized Commodity Description and Coding System (HS) supplies the common language. The HS is a classification system for goods that has been elaborated in the World Customs Organization (WCO), an international organization with headquarters in Brussels, Belgium. The function of the HS is to describe goods in a multilaterally agreed manner. Product descriptions are expressed in digits: the fewer the number of digits, the more generic the product category (for example, at the 2-digit level one might find the term "motor vehicles"); the higher the number of digits, the more specific the product category (for example, at the 8-digit level, one might find something like "passenger cars weighing less than 2 tons and with an engine not exceeding 1.5 liters, with a catalytic converter").

The HS plays a key role in the operation of the WTO as it defines the scheduling of tariff commitments (concessions) at the 6-digit level. While a number of WTO Members have formally not acceded to the international treaty establishing the HS, *de facto* all WTO Members follow the HS classification up to the 6-digit level. Beyond that, WTO Members are free to "shape" their tariff schedule, and thus their WTO concessions (tariff bindings) to their liking. Art. 3.3 of the HS Convention reads in this respect:

Nothing in this Article shall prevent a Contracting Party from establishing, in its Customs tariff or statistical nomenclatures, subdivisions classifying goods beyond the level of the Harmonized system, provided that any such subdivision is added and coded at a level beyond that of the six-digit numerical code set out in the Annex to this Convention.

By adding digits (disaggregating product categories), WTO Members cannot circumvent higher-level tariff bindings. Thus, a tariff at a more disaggregated level cannot be higher than the bound rate at the 6-digit or more aggregated level. An example from the US Tariff Schedule can help explain this point: Chapter 87 of the HS is entitled "Vehicles Other Than Railway Rolling-Stock, and Parts and Accessories Thereof." Heading 8708 is entitled "Parts and Accessories of the Motor Vehicles of Headings 8701 to 8705" (the two categories corresponding to tractors, motor vehicles for the transport of ten or more persons and motor cars principally designed for the transport of persons). Heading 8708.10 reads "Bumpers and Parts Thereof." Heading 8708.10.60 reads "Bumpers" (i.e., stampings). The United States bound their tariffs in Chapter 87 at the 8-digit level at 2.7 percent. This means that no tariff can be imposed on any 10- or 12-digit level that exceeds the maximum duty of 2.7 percent.

Periodically, the HS Committee of the WCO undertakes a review of the HS to take account of changes in technology and patterns in international trade and recommends certain amendments to the HS. The first of such changes came into force on 1 January 1992 (referred to as HS92). Another, more substantial change entered into force on 1 January 1996 (HS96). The WTO Committee on Tariff Concessions established simplified procedures to implement these changes and any future changes in the HS relating to GATT concessions (GATT Doc. BISD 39S/300). This was needed to reduce the administrative costs associated with remapping all the concessions made in the past.[4]

Non-discrimination with respect to customs duties amounts to the obligation (Art. I GATT) to treat goods of various origins (from any WTO Member) in an identical manner, that is, the customs treatment afforded by country A to, say, a car from country B should be equal to that afforded to a car originating in country C.[5] To respond to the question whether A is obliged to treat the two cars from countries B and C mentioned in our example above in an identical manner, the logic of the GATT requires that comparability between car B and car C is first established. This is where the notion of "likeness" kicks in. Likeness is far from being a self-interpreting term. GATT/WTO jurisprudence has had recourse to various criteria to establish likeness, but *tariff classification* is the dominant criterion. Thus, Members need to be sure that the tariff classification is sufficiently detailed. As a rule of thumb, tariff classifications at the 6-digit level seem to fit the bill in this respect, as WTO Members have the discretion to make tariff distinctions across substitutable products, to the extent that they come under different tariff lines. There is long line of case law in this respect.[6]

The 1978 panel report on *EEC – Animal Feed Proteins* concluded that "animal, marine and synthetic proteins were not products like those vegetable proteins covered by the [contested] measures" (§ 4.20).[7] Subsequently, a GATT panel on *Spain – Un-roasted Coffee* set aside the relevance of process-based distinctions when it comes to defining likeness. The case involved a complaint by Brazil regarding Spanish classification of un-roasted coffee, which distinguished between Colombian mild, other mild, unwashed Arabica, Robusta and other. The first two categories had duty-free treatment, while the last three were subject to a seven percent import duty. The duty for roasted coffee was unbound. Brazil argued this was inconsistent with Art. I GATT. The panel noted that:

> all arguments that had been advanced during the proceedings for the justification of a different tariff treatment for various groups and types of un-roasted coffee ... mainly related to organoleptic differences resulting from geographical factors, cultivation methods, the processing of the beans, and the genetic factor. The Panel did not consider that such differences were sufficient reason to allow for a different treatment.
>
> The Panel furthermore found relevant to its examination of the matter that un-roasted coffee was mainly, if not exclusively, sold in the form of blends, combining various types of coffee, and that coffee in its end-use, was universally regarded as a well-defined and single product intended for drinking.
>
> The Panel noted that no other contracting party applied its tariff regime in respect of un-roasted, non-decaffeinated coffee in such a way that different types of coffee were subject to different tariff rates.
>
> In light of the foregoing, the Panel *concluded* that un-roasted, non-decaffeinated coffee beans listed in the Spanish Customs Tariff ... should be considered as like products within the meaning of Article I.1.
>
> (§§ 4.7–4.10, italics in the original)

The panel report on *Japan – SPF Dimension Lumber* provides the most eloquent acknowledgment of the relevance of tariff classification as the dominant criterion to establish likeness:

> if a claim of likeness was raised by a contracting party in relation to the tariff treatment of its goods on importation by some other contracting party, such a claim should be based on the classification of the latter, i.e., the importing country's tariff.
>
> The Panel noted in this respect that "dimension lumber" as defined by Canada was a concept extraneous to the Japanese Tariff ... nor did it belong to any internationally accepted customs classification. The Panel concluded therefore that reliance by Canada on the concept of dimension lumber was not an appropriate basis for establishing "likeness" of products under Article I.1 of the General Agreement.
>
> (§§ 5.11–5.12)

Art. I GATT does not explicitly refer to either *de jure* or *de facto* discrimination. The Appellate Body clarified this issue in its report on *Canada – Autos* where in § 78 it notes:

> In approaching this question, we observe first that the words of Article I.1 do not restrict its scope only to cases in which the failure to accord an "advantage" to like products of all other Members appears *on the face* of the measure, or can be demonstrated on the basis of the words of the measure. Neither the words "*de jure*" nor "*de facto*" appear in Article I.1. Nevertheless, we observe that Article I.1 does not cover only "in law," or *de jure*, discrimination. As several GATT panel reports confirmed, Article I.1 covers also "in fact," or *de facto*, discrimination. Like the Panel, we cannot accept Canada's argument that Article I.1 does not apply to measures which, on their face, are "origin-neutral."

To establish a violation of Art. I GATT, a complainant need not show actual trade effects. It suffices that a WTO Member creates more favorable competitive *opportunities* for some WTO Members only, for a violation of Art. I GATT to be established.[8] Furthermore, the wording of Art. I GATT makes it clear that a WTO Member cannot treat imports from a non-WTO Member better than those of a WTO Member: in other words, imports from WTO Members will, in principle, receive the best possible treatment, hence the term most-favored-nation

(MFN) which reflects the non-discrimination principle when applied to customs duties and all other measures in connection with importation.

Of course, states may apply at the border measures other than customs duties. The Understanding on Art. II GATT distinguishes between "ordinary customs duties"[9] and "other duties and charges" and provides for the possibility that both categories of duties be bound (since the extent of tariff bindings is not a legal obligation but a matter of negotiation).[10] Second, other border practices and measures might affect imports: the time goods spend at the border, health inspections, etc. The MFN obligation covers any advantage in relation with importation and exportation of goods. The term "advantage" has been given a very wide coverage in GATT/WTO case law.

The MFN obligation moreover obliges WTO Members to extend any advantage (as understood above) immediately and unconditionally to all WTO Members. Whereas the first term seems to suggest the simple passage of time, the interpretation of the latter is an issue. The panel report on *Canada – Autos* (§§ 10.22 and 10.24) concluded that "unconditionally" means that a WTO Member cannot impose conditions beyond those imposed on the original beneficiary. It does not imply that it cannot impose any conditions at all. This report is particularly important for 8-digit classifications: in this line of thinking, a country which conditions benefits on, say, exports of textile goods upon satisfaction of specific labor standards, will not be violating MFN if it applies the mentioned condition on an MFN basis. Note that the legal value of this report remains uncertain because the AB vacated, albeit on other grounds, the panel report.

The panel report on *EC – Tariff Preferences* took a different route. It adopts a blanket prohibition on attaching any conditions as the proper way to understand the term "unconditionally":

> In the Panel's view, moreover, the term "unconditionally" in Article I.1 has a broader meaning than simply that of not requiring compensation. While the Panel acknowledges the European Communities' argument that conditionality in the context of traditional MFN clauses in bilateral treaties may relate to conditions of trade compensation for receiving MFN treatment, the Panel does not consider this to be the full meaning of "unconditionally" under Article I.1. Rather, the Panel sees no reason not to give that term its ordinary meaning under Article I.1, that is, "not limited by or subject to any conditions." Because the tariff preferences under the Drug Arrangements are accorded only on the condition that the receiving countries are experiencing a certain gravity of

drug problems, these tariff preferences are not accorded "unconditionally" to the like products originating in all other WTO Members, as required by Article I:1. The Panel therefore finds that the tariff advantages under the Drug Arrangements are not consistent with Article I:1 of GATT 1994.

(§§ 7.59–7.60)

This makes sense when dealing with tariff lines up to the 6-digit level, where description of goods is harmonized. It is still an open question, however, whether this line of thinking is reconcilable with the contractual freedom that WTO Members in principle have to draft their own 8-digit-level classifications. As things stand, there is no definitive answer to this question.[11]

The treatment of quantitative restrictions

Import and export quantitative restrictions (QRs) are illegal *per se*. Even non-discriminatory QRs violate Art. XI GATT, since there is no discrimination-test embedded in Art. XI GATT. The term QR is not self-interpreting. Duties and taxes cannot be considered QRs, nor can domestic measures that are enforced at the border (Interpretative Note ad Art. III). For example, a ban on sales of asbestos containing materials that is enforced at the border, if challenged, will be adjudicated under Art. III GATT, not Art. XI GATT.

WTO case law has opted for defining the term QR to cover not only cases where a numerical target has been set, but any QR-*equivalent* measure. The GATT panel report on *Japan – Semiconductors* established the wide coverage of Art. XI GATT. It held for the proposition that when a government provides *incentives* to private parties to act in a manner inconsistent with Art. XI GATT, such behavior is GATT-inconsistent. In the semiconductor case, Japanese firms raised prices (which led to reduced exports) as a result of incentives (including administrative guidance and monitoring of costs and prices) by the Japanese government. This report is important in two distinct ways: first, showing that measures which are not strictly speaking quantitative restrictions but result in reduction of trade, are covered by Art. XI GATT; and, second, that government actions that do not *require* (mandate) a specific behavior of private parties, but do provide incentives to do so, can be caught by Art. XI GATT.

This panel report has been cited by all subsequent reports dealing with the interpretation of Art. XI GATT. Thus, it is now settled case law that the term QR covers not only *de jure* quantitative restrictions (numerical limits or targets) but also *de facto* QRs (anything which might operate as a QR), irrespective whether the subject of the challenged activity is the state or the private sector. However, for private actions to be captured by the prohibition enshrined in Art. XI GATT, they must be *attributed* to a government. The degree of intervention for attribution to the state is quite low: incentives suffice.

Summing up all subsequent case law on this issue, the panel report on *Argentina – Hides and Leather* went on to state:

> It is well established in GATT/WTO jurisprudence that only governmental measures fall within the ambit of Article XI.1. This said, we recall the statement of the panel in *Japan – Measures Affecting Consumer Photographic Film and Paper* to the effect that:
> [P]ast GATT cases demonstrate that the fact that an action is taken by private parties does not rule out the possibility that it may be deemed governmental if there is sufficient governmental involvement with it. It is difficult to establish bright-line rules in this regard, however. Thus, that possibility will need to be examined on a case-by-case basis.
>
> (§ 11.18, italics in the original)

The same report, however, provided an important clarification in this respect. In its view, a government measure providing incentives to act in an Art. XI GATT-inconsistent manner, should be dissociated from a measure which does not eliminate all potential for such behavior. This was probably the first attempt to reduce the scope of the ruling in *Japan – Semiconductors*:

> We agree with the view expressed by the panel in *Japan – Film*. However, we do not think that it follows either from that panel's statement or from the text or context of Article XI:1 that Members are under an obligation to exclude any possibility that governmental measures may enable private parties, directly or indirectly, to restrict trade, where those measures themselves are not trade-restrictive.
>
> (§ 11.19)

In the same report, the panel established the standard of review applicable in Art. XI GATT cases. The panel distinguishes between *de jure* and *de facto* QRs. With respect to the latter, the panel stated that, for a successful legal challenge to be mounted, the complainant must demonstrate a causal link between the measure attacked and the (reduced) level of trade. This attempt to reduce the scope of the ruling in *Japan – Semiconductors* gives rise to the question how to demonstrate the required link absent some form of effects test. Without addressing in detail the case of a *de jure* QR, the panel made it implicitly clear that the evidentiary standard should be lower in such cases:

> [I]t should be recalled that Article XI.1, like Articles I, II and III of the GATT 1994, protects competitive opportunities of imported products, not trade flows. In order to establish that [the measure] infringes Article XI.1, the European Communities need not prove actual trade effects. However, it must be borne in mind that [the measure] is alleged by the European Communities to make effective a *de facto* rather than a *de jure* restriction. In such circumstances, it is inevitable, as an evidentiary matter, that greater weight attaches to the actual trade impact of a measure.
>
> Even if it emerges from trade statistics that the level of exports is unusually low, this does not prove, in and of itself, that that level is attributable, in whole or in part, to the measure alleged to constitute an export restriction. Particularly in the context of an alleged *de facto* restriction and where, as here, there are possibly multiple restrictions, it is necessary for a complaining party to establish a causal link between the contested measure and the low level of exports. In our view, whatever else it may involve, a demonstration of causation must consist of a persuasive explanation of precisely how the measure at issue causes or contributes to the low level of exports.
>
> (§§ 11.21 and 11.22)

The claim by the European Community, the complainant in this case, was that the presence of representatives of the domestic industry at customs clearance procedures, sufficed to establish a QR, since, it was in the interest of the domestic industry not to allow exports of hides from the Argentine market. The panel, based on the grounds mentioned immediately supra, rejected this claim, arguing that the presence of representatives of the domestic industry does not suffice for establishing a violation of Art. XI GATT.

> We agree that it is unusual to have representatives from a downstream consuming industry involved in the Customs process of export clearance. As noted above, it seems to us that the levels of exports of raw hides from Argentina may be low. The European

Communities has stated the matter to us in the form of a rhetorical question – what other purpose could these downstream industry representatives have in this government process of export clearance than restricting exports? However, it is up to the European Communities to provide evidence sufficient to convince us of that. In this instance, we do not find that the evidence is sufficient to prove that there is an export restriction made effective by the mere presence of tanners' representatives within the meaning of Article XI.

(§ 7.35)

This panel report was not appealed, so it is not known if the AB would concur. As things stand, the *Japan – Semiconductors* case law should not be disregarded.

Internal measures: national treatment

The national treatment obligation (Art. III GATT) appears right after Art. II GATT (consolidation of customs duties), indicating that Art. III GATT becomes legally relevant only once imports have paid the "entry ticket" into a particular market (in the form of customs duties). The national treatment obligation is needed because virtually all domestic policy instruments are left unconstrained in the WTO, potentially leaving the parties with plenty of scope to undo tariff bindings. In order to limit the scope for this, tariff bindings are complemented with an obligation not to discriminate between domestic and foreign products once the latter have entered a given market. The purpose of Art. III GATT is thus to prevent "concession erosion" through the discriminatory application of domestic policies.

National treatment is a cost-effective defense against opportunistic (protectionist) use of domestic policy instruments to circumvent tariff bindings. The essential function of the national treatment instrument is to make domestic measures *blunter instruments of protection*. In the case of taxation, the more "fine tuned" tax policy instruments governments have at their disposal, the more tempting it will be for them to pursue beggar-thy-neighbor policies. If all (like) domestic products have to be burdened with the higher taxes imposed on imported products, taxes become a less attractive instrument of protection.[12]

As noted in the AB report on *Japan – Alcoholic Beverages II* (p. 16):

The broad and fundamental purpose of Article III is to avoid protectionism in the application of internal tax and regulatory measures. More specifically, the purpose of Article III "is to ensure that internal measures 'not be applied to imported or domestic products so as to afford protection to domestic production.'" Toward this end, Article III obliges Members of the WTO to provide equality of competitive conditions for imported products in relation to domestic products.

The coverage of the national treatment obligation in positive law

The national treatment obligation extends to both bound and unbound tariff lines. The wording of Art. III GATT does not explicitly address this point. The AB in its report on *Japan – Alcoholic Beverages II* eliminated any remaining doubt as to the coverage of Art. III GATT in the following terms:

> The Article III national treatment obligation is a general prohibition on the use of internal taxes and other internal regulatory measures so as to afford protection to domestic production. This obligation clearly extends also to products not bound under Article II.

It follows that the obligation not to discriminate in favor of domestic products is legalese for the obligation not to protect domestic production. The term *protection*, however, lends itself to different interpretations and, as things stand, we still lack an operational definition of this term.

Art. III GATT extends to regulatory interventions of both a fiscal (Art. III.2 GATT), and non-fiscal nature (Art. III.4 GATT). A fiscal imposition on goods affects trade by modifying the price of the good concerned. This explains why Art. III.2 GATT (which covers fiscal measures) does not include the words "affecting trade," whereas these words are found in Art. III.4 GATT (covering non-fiscal measures). In contrast to European Community disciplines on free movement of goods – where over time the coverage of analogous disciplines has been reduced to avoid punishing behavior that has minimal or unintended/tangential impacts on the free movement of goods,[13] WTO adjudicating bodies interpret the term "affecting" very widely. To date, there has never been a case which has failed the "affecting" threshold in the context of Art. III GATT litigation.

Two policy measures are explicitly exempted from the national treatment obligation by virtue of Art. III.8 GATT: subsidies and government procurement. The treatment of the former is regulated in a separate multilateral agreement, the *WTO Agreement on Subsidies and Countervailing Measures* (SCM). This Agreement defines subsidies as government schemes that grant benefits to specific entities. It further divides subsidies into actionable and prohibited. The latter comprise explicit export subsidies (Art. 4 SCM). The former are defined by default: any scheme which is attributed to government and confers a benefit to a specific entity and which is not a prohibited subsidy is an actionable subsidy.

The classification of subsidies has important legal ramifications. There is an overlap in the defense against prohibited and actionable subsidies: importing WTO Members can unilaterally impose (subject to the disciplines of SCM in this respect) countervailing duties against them up to the amount of the subsidy paid. There is a divergence as well: WTO Members can request that the subsidizing Member withdraw a prohibited subsidy or withdraw/modify an actionable subsidy. In case of non-compliance, the injured WTO Member will be allowed to take countermeasures against the subsidizing state up to the amount of the subsidy paid (in case of prohibited subsidy) or up to the amount of the injury suffered (in case of an actionable subsidy). Injury is defined as injury to the producer producing the "like" (that is, competing in the same relevant product market) good. By embedding an injury to competitors' standard, the SCM excludes (as a matter of legal obligation) any inquiry into the welfare implications of subsidization – that is, the objective of the subsidizing government is irrelevant, as is the effectiveness of the instrument in attaining the underlying objective.

Exclusion from the national treatment obligation for procurement essentially means that WTO Members do not have to abide by the national treatment obligation when government entities purchase goods without the intention to re-sell. In light of the importance of the government procurement market but also the unwillingness of many WTO Members to limit their discretion in this respect, a sub-set of WTO Members entered into a plurilateral agreement (i.e., binding only the signatories) whereby they essentially re-introduced the national treatment obligation for all purchases of entities listed in their respective schedules of concessions.[14]

Establishing a violation of national treatment

In light of the divergent wording in GATT Art. III.2 (fiscal) and Art. III.4 (other internal policies), the legal test for violation of the national treatment obligation usually treats fiscal and non-fiscal measures separately. There is, however, an emerging jurisprudential approach that is premised on the view that Art. III.1 GATT discourages the protectionist use of domestic legislation *irrespective* of whether fiscal or non-fiscal measures are used.

The national treatment obligation requires a double comparison: the treatment of foreign goods may not be less advantageous than that accorded to domestic like goods (the national treatment angle) and the most favored treatment with respect to internal measures accorded to one foreign product must immediately and unconditionally be accorded to all like foreign products (the MFN angle). As a result, the treatment accorded to domestic products must be accorded to *all* foreign like products.

For a violation of Art. III GATT to occur, a successful complainant has to establish that a WTO Member has intervened through regulatory means so as to afford protection to domestic competing (like) products. Hence, the complainant must persuade the WTO adjudicating body that the product pair at hand (domestic–foreign) are *like* and that the measure challenged treats the domestic product in a more advantageous manner. Relevant GATT/WTO case law has clarified that for likeness to be determined: (1) demand-side factors are relevant; (2) econometric or other indicators may be used; and (3) all like products have to be directly competitive or substitutable.[15]

An influential GATT-era case was *Border Tax Adjustments*[16] where a Working Party report defined criteria to establish likeness, or if products are directly competitive or substitutable:

> Some criteria were suggested for determining, on a case-by-case basis, whether a product is "similar": the product's end-uses in a given market; consumers' tastes and habits, which change from country to country; the product's properties, nature and quality.
>
> (§ 18)

The AB reports on *Japan – Alcoholic Beverages II* and on *Korea – Alcoholic Beverages* have excluded supply-side criteria in establishing likeness; they limit the relevant criteria to the demand side in the marketplace. While the first report attempts to apply standard economic criteria such as the cross-price elasticity in determining likeness, the second report allows complainants to use other criteria such as physical characteristics, consumer preferences and end-uses. In *EC – Asbestos*, the AB implicitly adopted a "*reasonable consumer*" test, holding that consumers, knowing of the danger that asbestos represents to health, would always privilege asbestos-free construction material over products containing asbestos. An implication is that there was no need to look for evidence in the market to confirm this presumption (§ 117). From an economic perspective, looking at demand side characteristics only does not make much sense.

For products to be like, they have to share some properties beyond what two directly competitive or substitutable products share. So far, WTO case law has offered one such extra property: customs classification (the AB report on *Japan – Alcoholic Beverages II*). Hence, two directly competitive or substitutable products which come under the same HS classification[17] are considered to be like.

In *EC – Asbestos*, the AB held that the four criteria to evaluate likeness (physical properties, end uses, consumer perceptions and tariff classification) mentioned in the GATT Working Party report on *Border Tax Adjustments* are simply tools that must be examined together by panels since they are inter-related. That is, panels should examine all pertinent evidence before them as they provide a framework for analyzing the "likeness" of particular products on a case-by-case basis (§ 102 of the report). The same report also argues that physical characteristics require a separate examination as the extent to which products share common physical properties may be a useful indicator of "likeness," and noted that:

> There will be few situations where the evidence on the "likeness" of products will lend itself to "clear results." In many cases, the evidence will give conflicting indications, possibly within each of the four criteria. For instance, there may be some evidence of similar physical properties and some evidence of differing physical properties. Or the physical properties may differ completely, yet there may be strong evidence of similar end-uses and a high degree of substitutability of the products from the perspective of the consumer. A panel cannot decline to inquire into relevant evidence simply because it suspects that evidence may not be "clear" or, for that matter, because the parties agree that certain evidence is not relevant.
>
> Furthermore, in a case such as this, where the fibres are physically very different, a panel *cannot* conclude that they are "like products" if it *does not examine* evidence relating to consumers' tastes and habits. In such a situation, if there is *no* inquiry into this aspect of the nature and extent of the competitive relationship between the products, there is no basis for overcoming the

inference, drawn from the different physical properties of the products, that the products are not "like."

(emphasis in the original)

As a result, in this case, the AB found that asbestos-containing construction material and asbestos-free construction material are unlike products for the purposes of Art. III.4 GATT. Thus, the AB acknowledged a pre-eminent role in the *physical characteristics* criterion.

Regulation so as to afford protection

A key condition for a measure to violate national treatment is that it has the effect of affording protection. This is probably one of the weakest areas in GATT/WTO jurisprudence, reflecting the absence of a clear operational definition of the term protection. Many adjudicating bodies (and more recently, legislators as well) use proxies in order to establish whether protection has indeed been accorded through a regulation. However, the WTO case law in this field is ambiguous.

With respect to fiscal policies, Art. III.2 GATT requests that foreign products: (1) should not be taxed in excess of like domestic products, whereas (2) they should not be taxed in a manner that affords protection to domestic directly competitive or substitutable products. The key term in (1) is *in excess*. This has been equated in case law to a pure arithmetic difference in taxation irrespective of the margin (for violation, of course, to occur, the more burdensome taxation must be imposed on the foreign product). For a violation of (2) to occur, the tax differential must be more than *de minimis* (with this to be determined on a case-by-case basis).

When it comes to non-fiscal measures, Art. III.4 GATT imposes an obligation not to accord to imported products less favorable treatment than that accorded to domestic like products. The AB in *EC – Asbestos* acknowledged that:

[B]y interpreting the term "like products" in Article III.4 in this way, we give that provision a relatively broad product scope – although no broader than the product scope of Article III.2. In so doing, we observe that there is a second element that must be established before a measure can be held to be inconsistent with Article III.4. Thus, even if two products are "like," that does not mean that a measure is inconsistent with Article III.4. A complaining Member must still establish that the measure accords to the group of "like" *imported* products "less favorable treatment" than it accords to the group of "like" *domestic* products. The term "less favorable treatment" expresses the general principle, in Article III.1, that internal regulations "should not be applied ... so as to afford protection to domestic production." If there is "less favorable treatment" of the group of "like" imported products, there is, conversely, "protection" of the group of "like" domestic products. However, a Member may draw distinctions between products which have been found to be "like," without, for this reason alone, according to the group of "like" *imported* products "less favorable treatment" than that accorded to the group of "like" *domestic* products.

(§ 100, emphasis in the original)

To establish whether a regulation operates in a protectionist manner, a successful complainant does not have to show either protective effects or protective intent. The GATT panel report on *US – Superfund* had clarified that Art. III protects expectations as to particular behavior and not actual trade outcomes. In these terms, the *US – Superfund* panel dismissed an argument by the United States that its discriminatory taxation scheme did not constitute a violation of Art. III since the effects on the market were negligible in light of the minor tax differential. The AB in its report on *Japan – Alcoholic Beverages II* reaffirmed this conclusion, and held for the proposition that intent is immaterial for the purposes of establishing a violation of Art. III GATT.

In a nutshell, trade effects and/or regulatory intent do not matter when determining whether a regulatory intervention operates so as to afford protection. Moreover, likeness or direct comparability/substitutability may be established through various means or criteria. This flexibility can have implications in determining what is permissible under Art. III GATT. From an institutional perspective, undue intrusion in the exercise of regulatory autonomy can weaken the support for multilateral rules. Unfortunately, this is precisely what the above-described case law has achieved. WTO adjudicating bodies have outlawed legislation with unproven protectionist effect and probably with no protectionist intent at all.

An example is a case involving a Chilean law that distinguished between three categories of alcoholic beverages: drinks below 35° alcoholic content; drinks between 35° and 39°; and finally drinks with alcoholic content of more than 39°. The products in the first category were taxed at 27 percent *ad valorem* whereas those in the last one were taxed at 47 percent *ad valorem*. The complaining parties argued that some imported products of slightly more than 39° were directly comparable to Chilean products of less than 35° and that the tax differential operated so as to afford protection to these products. Chile responded that the majority of the affected products were domestic and that no protection could therefore result (§ 58). The AB report on *Chile – Alcoholic Beverages* agreed with the factual observation, but dismissed its relevance in the following terms:

> This fact does not, however, by itself outweigh the other relevant factors, which tend to reveal the protective application of the New Chilean System. The relative proportion of domestic versus imported products within a particular fiscal category is not, in and of itself, decisive of the appropriate characterization of the total impact of the New Chilean system under Article III:2, second sentence, of the GATT 1994. This provision, as noted earlier, provides for equality of competitive conditions of *all* directly competitive or substitutable imported products, in relation to domestic products, and not simply, as Chile argues, those imported products within a particular fiscal category. The cumulative consequence of the New Chilean System is, as the Panel found, that approximately 75 percent of all domestic production of the distilled alcoholic beverages at issue will be located in the fiscal category with the lowest tax rate, whereas approximately 95 percent of the directly competitive or substitutable imported products will be found in the fiscal category subject to the highest tax rate.
>
> (§ 67, italics in the original)

As a result, Chile was requested to defend its policies under Art. XX GATT (the exceptions provision – see below). Chile decided not to do so, and consequently, it was requested to bring its fiscal regime into conformity with the multilateral rules. Recourse to Art. XX GATT (discussed below) is no panacea, as the burden of proof shifts to the regulating state. On the other hand, GATT/WTO case law has consistently construed the list of exceptions figuring in Art. XX GATT as exhaustive. As a result, regulatory distinctions on grounds other than those mentioned in that list (e.g., luxury taxes) risk being outlawed even though such distinctions might not be accompanied by protectionist intent or effect.

The AB conclusion in the Chilean case illustrates the need to re-think the interpretation of Art. III. The national treatment obligation was originally designed as an instrument for *non-discrimination* and not as an instrument for *de-regulation*. Yet, such will be occasionally the outcome, as for example in our luxury taxes scenario, were one to follow the now dominant interpretation of Art. III GATT. To our mind, the WTO adjudicating bodies were led to this situation because their focus is not on the over-arching function of Art. III GATT: to combat protectionism. While protection is an elusive concept, sometimes quite obvious and sometimes quite hard to detect, the credibility of WTO adjudicating bodies will, in important part, be judged by reference to the internal consistency of their decisions. A key ingredient of such consistency is some sort of a theory/understanding of what protection might mean. And this is precisely what has been missing in case law so far.

The "new generation" WTO agreements (such as the *Agreement on Technical Barriers to Trade* (TBT), and the *Agreement on Sanitary and Phytosanitary Measures* (SPS)) are, in this context, less troublesome in the sense that they reflect more elaborate understandings of the non-discrimination obligation. A domestic regulation can simultaneously fall under the Art. III GATT, the TBT and/or the SPS agreements. If this is the case, then the SPS prevails by virtue of Art. 1.5 TBT (which establishes that the SPS takes precedence over the TBT) and because the *EC – Asbestos* jurisprudence establishes that the TBT takes precedence over the GATT.

According to the TBT agreement, a WTO Member enacting a technical regulation or standard (as defined in the TBT) must respect the national treatment obligation (assuming no relevant international standard exists, which, in principle, must be followed according to Art. 2.4 TBT) and will further have to ensure that its legislation is *necessary* for it to achieve its unilaterally set regulatory objective. Necessity in this context means that WTO Members are free to pursue any objective they deem appropriate but at the same time have to choose the means that will have the least possible negative repercussions on international trade while pursuing this objective. Necessity does not oblige WTO Members to target their objectives in the sense that they must always use the first-best instrument to realize a social preference. It does go some way towards this direction, however, since the underlying assumption of this principle is that the most onerous of international trade measures will not be utilized. Hence, necessity emerges as a proxy relevant in the investigation whether or not protection was indeed intended and/or provided.

The SPS Agreement goes even further in this respect. Besides what has been described above, the SPS Agreement obliges WTO Members to base their interventions on scientific evidence and a process of risk assessment (only if there is no relevant scientific evidence may governments invoke the so-called "precautionary" principle) and also to

ensure some coherence (Art. 5.5 SPS) in their health- and/or environmental policies. Science and policy coherence are additional proxies
that could help distinguish wheat from chaff and enable adjudicating
bodies to minimize both false positives and negatives. Of course, the
system is still far from providing a "one size fits all" solution in this
context. But some significant steps in the right direction were taken
when enacting the TBT and SPS Agreements.

A brief summary

To sum up our discussion so far, adherence to the WTO contract
implies a ban on the use of QRs, an obligation (the extent of which
depends on domestic preferences and international negotiations) to
consolidate customs duties (and thus avoid volatility which in this
respect is synonymous to increased transaction costs), and an obligation to avoid two forms of subsidization (pecuniary, with respect to
export subsidies, and regulatory by virtue of the national treatment
provision). Otherwise, WTO Members are essentially free to unilaterally
pursue trade policies, subject to the constraint that national regulators
do not discriminate between domestic and foreign like goods. This
limited reach reflects the intentions of the founders of the GATT to
limit their cooperation to so-called "negative integration," as opposed
to more far-reaching positive integration (harmonized policies).

Since we still live in a world with import duties, the role of national
treatment in its current, *static* dimension is to ensure that the value of
negotiated concessions are not undermined through unilateral policies.
Eventually however, we will move to a world without customs duties.
This does not necessarily entail that WTO Members will lose the
incentive to pursue beggar-thy-neighbor policies through instruments
other than customs duties. Indeed, this is exactly what internal fiscal
and non-fiscal instruments can achieve. In its *dynamic* dimension, the
national treatment obligation might have to be re-evaluated and re-
drafted. In a tariff-free world, internal *non-discriminatory* instruments
might prove to be a formidable obstacle to trade liberalization.[18] A
dynamic approach towards national treatment might lead to interna
tional negotiations that focus on the efficiency of domestic policies,
that is, go beyond the existing parameters of non-discrimination.

State contingencies

A WTO Member can deviate from its default commitments by invoking one of the state contingencies provided for under the WTO or by

re-negotiating its commitments. There are many provisions in the GATT that allow for deviations from the basic (default) obligations (i.e., binding of customs duties, prohibition of QRs, non-discrimination). We classify them into three categories:

1 *Industry state contingencies*: measures inconsistent with basic WTO obligations that reflect a desire to assist specific industries in competing with imports – the focus here is solely on a subset of society: domestic producers.
2 *Economy-wide*: policies aimed at a macroeconomic problem or delivery of a public good (e.g., health, safety) – in contrast to (1), the primary objective here is to enhance overall welfare.
3 *Institutional* (*systemic*): measures motivated by a desire on the part of the membership as a whole to address a country-specific issue or to safeguard the functioning of the trading system as a whole.

Industry (state contingencies)

Under "industry," we classify five legal instruments: antidumping, countervailing, safeguards, infant industry protection, and re-negotiation of customs duties.[19] The first three are customarily referred to in literature as "contingent protection" instruments, since protection can be activated upon occurrence of a particular contingency (dumping, subsidization or increased imports, respectively). Infant industry protection, on the other hand, will occur depending on the decision of the WTO Member concerned with the development of one particular sector and not upon the occurrence of an *exogenous* contingency. The same is true for re-negotiation of bound customs duties: a WTO Member can request either at a pre-agreed period or at any time a re-balancing of its customs protection. All five instruments principally aim at protecting domestic producer interests.

Antidumping (AD)

The WTO does not forbid dumping, i.e., the practice of an exporter selling output in export markets at a price that is less than what the firm charges in its domestic or home market. Dumping as such is not illegal.[20] WTO Members *have the right but not the obligation* to take action against it. If they do, they must abide by the WTO *Agreement on Antidumping* (AD). The focus of this agreement is on the legality of imposition of AD duties. The AD agreement lays out detailed procedural criteria that must be followed by national enforcement bodies.

Antidumping duties may only be imposed following an investigation that establishes that dumping has occurred and that it has caused material injury to the domestic producer producing the like product. The dumping margin does not have to reflect actual prices: the AD Agreement allows investigating authorities to avail themselves of the possibility to "construct" the home market price (in AD parlance, the normal value) in cases where the alleged "dumper" does not cooperate or when the sales of the firms concerned in their home market are below a certain threshold. The injury standard is limited to injury to direct competitors only. Some domestic statutes include "public interest" clauses that require (allow) investigating authorities to determine what the impact of taking an AD action would be on users of imports – this is not, however, a WTO requirement. The AD Agreement imposes a ceiling on the magnitude of AD duties: these can never surpass the dumping margin found during the investigation.[21] AD duties have to lapse after five years (sunset clause) unless, during a review conducted to this effect, it is shown that their elimination would be likely to lead to continuation or recurrence of dumping and injury.

AD duties are an exception to Art. I (MFN) in the sense that exporters (firms) found to be dumping will be paying more (confront higher duties) to enter into a particular market than non-dumpers. Note that AD duties are firm-specific, as margins are calculated at the level of the exporting firm. They need not take the form of duties – many countries negotiate undertakings with the affected exporters under which they agree to reduce their exports or increase prices in the export market. In such cases exporters will be able to capture some rents that otherwise would have gone to the importing country's treasury. Note also that although AD duties are a border measure, functionally AD is derived from (based on) competition law, in that the purported rationale is to combat predation.[22] In practice, most analysts and even most practitioners would agree that predation is no longer a motivating force for AD, if it ever was – AD is simple protectionism. However, this is the only conceptually valid rationale for AD. If so, it can be pointed out that they are a deviation from Art. III GATT on the basis of the *Kodak-Fuji* jurisprudence – which accepted that competition laws come under the coverage of Art. III GATT.

Countervailing duties (CVDs) and subsidies

The WTO *Agreement on Subsidies and Countervailing Measures (SCM)* regulates both the granting of subsidies and the conditions under which CVDs may be imposed. CVDs are duties imposed on subsidized imports upon importation. Necessary conditions for the use of CVDs are that an investigation determines that subsidies have been granted, and that the subsidies have caused material injury to domestic producers producing the like product. CVDs must lapse after five years (sunset clause) unless a review demonstrates that their elimination would be likely to lead to continuation or recurrence of subsidization and injury. As discussed above, subsidies are an exception to the National Treatment obligation as per Art. III.8 GATT.

A subsidy is defined as any measure that has a cost to government and that confers a benefit to a *specific* addressee. A distinction is made between prohibited and actionable subsidies.[23] The former comprise *export* subsidies (paid contingent upon the exportation of the subsidized good) and *local content* subsidies (paid if part of the added value is of national origin). These two types of subsidies are illegal. If a panel finds they have been granted, the subsidizing Member must withdraw them immediately. All other subsidies are actionable.

Members affected by subsidies can either impose CVDs or challenge the prohibited or actionable character of the subsidy. They cannot at the same time impose CVDs *and* countermeasures (retaliation under Art. 22 DSU, see below), in cases where a Member has not withdrawn its subsidy. CVDs provide instant "relief," that is, duties will be imposed to counteract the effects of a subsidy at the end of the investigation process (usually one year). Attacking a subsidy, however, is a substantially lengthier process. In general, large countries that confront subsidized imports have a choice between investigating the subsidies and imposing CVDs or attack the subsidy before a panel.[24] Smaller countries tend to be disadvantaged insofar as subsidies disproportionately displace their exports on third markets. In such cases, they cannot use the CVD weapon. This helps to explain the emphasis on the part of major agricultural exporters such as Australia, Brazil, Argentina and New Zealand on negotiating disciplines on the use of agricultural subsidies.

Safeguards

The WTO *Agreement on Safeguards (SGA)* allows Members, when faced with increased imports that cause serious injury to the domestic producer, to temporarily raise customs duties (safeguards are, thus, an exception to Art. II GATT – the tariff bindings), to impose a QR (safeguards are thus an exception to Art. XI GATT), or to impose a tariff rate quota (TRQ). The existence of safeguard provisions in trade agreements facilitates negotiation of liberalization commitments by providing some insurance that countries can impose protection temporarily if an industry is having problems adjusting to increased competition from imports.

The WTO requires that safeguards cannot be imposed for a period of more than four years and may only be renewed once for an equivalent period. Every imposition of safeguards must be followed by an equally lengthy "peace clause" (e.g., if country A imposes a safeguard on steel for four years and they do not wish to renew it, they may not impose another safeguard on steel for the years immediately following the period of safeguard imposition).

A major difference between safeguards and AD/CVD is that safeguards must respect the MFN obligation, that is, they must affect equally all imports of the goods concerned, no matter what the source. In contrast, AD/CVD are country-specific. In addition, AD often is firm-specific as the dumping margin will depend on the pricing strategy of the firms (and the methodology used by the authorities). A common form of safeguard used in the 1980s was the voluntary export restraint (VER) – a negotiated country-specific limit on exports of particular products. These are WTO illegal.[25] In order to satisfy the MFN obligation, the SGA specifies that if safeguards take the form of quotas, these be allocated to affected exporters proportionately to their pre-existing market shares. However, they can *modulate* the allocation of quotas by "hitting" exporters whose exports have grown in a disproportionate manner harder. In principle, a country imposing safeguards must compensate affected WTO Member(s) by lowering its customs duties in goods of export interest to those Member(s). However, this obligation only applies if safeguards are imposed for more than three years.

All the contingent protection options discussed above impose a causality standard – imports must have caused injury. This has been criticized by many economists. There are many factors that give rise to adjustment pressures ("injury"), not just imports. Examples are changes in consumer tastes or technologies. An implication is that the appropriate government response to injury of industry involves general adjustment policies that apply independent of the cause of injury. In addition to the weak economics, careless case law has failed to define an internally coherent approach to adjudicating disputes.[26]

Infant industry protection

Art. XVIIIc GATT allows WTO Members to use trade policies that would otherwise violate tariff commitments or the ban on quotas to facilitate the establishment, or the promotion, of a particular industry (infant industry protection). Only developing countries (as defined in Art. XVIII.4 GATT) may invoke this possibility. A necessary condition for the imposition of such measures is that affected exporters are compensated. The provision has not been used frequently, both because of this compensation requirement and because developing countries have either had high tariff bindings or not bound tariffs at all for goods produced locally, obviating the need to invoke Art. XVIIIc.

Re-negotiation of customs duties

The foregoing four provisions allow for temporary increases in protection. In practice, a government may want to increase protection on a longer-term basis. GATT Art. XXVIII allows for this through renegotiation of tariff bindings. This involves negotiations to reduce other tariffs so that affected WTO Members are compensated. To facilitate the negotiation process, Art. XXVIII limits the number of participants to those who initially negotiated the tariff binding. Under the WTO, in addition to countries that have such initial negotiating rights (INRs), countries can have a "principal supplying" or a "substantial" interest (defined as having market shares larger than those of the INR countries in the import market concerned – see the Interpretative Note ad Art. XXVIII GATT). These countries will collectively determine the set of products on which duties must be lowered.

Assuming successful conclusion of negotiations, the new rates must be notified and applied on an MFN basis. If no agreement obtains, the State seeking to change its protection may still do so. In such cases, Art. XXVIII GATT does not adequately define the ambit of the permissible response by affected exporters. For example, following the EU enlargement in 1995, Sweden, Finland and Austria had to raise some of their duties to the EC level. In subsequent negotiations, no agreement emerged, and Canada threatened to retaliate. In the event, it did not do so, so it is still an open issue what the permissible response is in case of disagreement.[27]

Economy-wide provisions

There are three major provisions: (1) general economic (Art. XII and XVIIIb GATT); (2) public order (Art. XX GATT); and (3) national security exceptions (Art. XXI GATT).

Balance of payments

GATT Articles XII (for industrialized countries) and XVIIIb (for developing countries) permit the use of trade restrictions to safeguard a country's external financial position. The inclusion of these provisions reflects the system of fixed exchange rates that prevailed when the GATT/ITO was originally negotiated. Under fixed exchange rates a country with a payments deficit cannot devalue easily. As import restrictions (in conjunction with export subsidies) are equivalent to a nominal devaluation, allowing (temporary) import barriers to deal with a balance of payments can make sense. Since 1948 most countries have shifted to flexible exchange rates. Given that the exchange rate is a more appropriate instrument to deal with balance of payment disequilibria – as part of a comprehensive macroeconomic adjustment program – these GATT provisions have largely become redundant.

During much of the GATT years, developing countries made frequent use of Art. XVIIIb as cover for the use of QRs. During the Uruguay Round, the scope to use QRs under Art. XVIIIb was reduced and surveillance strengthened. In principle, surcharges or similar measures must be applied on an across-the-board basis – as that is what is needed from a balance of payments (BOP) perspective. A panel for a high profile case brought by the US in 1997 against India – which justified QRs on over 2,700 agricultural and industrial product tariff lines – found India's measures to be inconsistent with GATT Articles XI.1 and XVIII.11 and nullified or impaired benefits accruing to the US under the Agreement on Agriculture. Most importantly, the panel found (and the AB upheld) that BOP restrictions can be the subject matter of judicial review.

Public order

Art. XX GATT contains a list of grounds that justify deviations from the GATT obligations. It reads:

> Subject to the requirement that such measures are not applied in a manner which would constitute a means of arbitrary or unjustifiable discrimination between countries where the same conditions prevail, or a disguised restriction on international trade, nothing in this Agreement shall be construed to prevent the adoption or enforcement by any contracting party of measures:
>
> (a) necessary to protect public morals;
> (b) necessary to protect human, animal or plant life or health;

(c) relating to the importations or exportations of gold or silver;

(d) necessary to secure compliance with laws or regulations which are not inconsistent with the provisions of this Agreement, including those relating to customs enforcement, the enforcement of monopolies operated under paragraph 4 of Article II and Article XVII, the protection of patents, trade marks and copyrights, and the prevention of deceptive practices;

(e) relating to the products of prison labor;

(f) imposed for the protection of national treasures of artistic, historic or archaeological value;

(g) relating to the conservation of exhaustible natural resources if such measures are made effective in conjunction with restrictions on domestic production or consumption;

(h) undertaken in pursuance of obligations under any intergovernmental commodity agreement which conforms to criteria submitted to the CONTRACTING PARTIES and not disapproved by them or which is itself so submitted and not so disapproved;

(i) involving restrictions on exports of domestic materials necessary to ensure essential quantities of such materials to a domestic processing industry during periods when the domestic price of such materials is held below the world price as part of a governmental stabilization plan; *Provided* that such restrictions shall not operate to increase the exports of or the protection afforded to such domestic industry, and shall not depart from the provisions of this Agreement relating to non-discrimination;

(j) essential to the acquisition or distribution of products in general or local short supply; *Provided* that any such measures shall be consistent with the principle that all contracting parties are entitled to an equitable share of the international supply of such products, and that any such measures, which are inconsistent with the other provisions of the Agreement shall be discontinued as soon as the conditions giving rise to them have ceased to exist. The CONTRACTING PARTIES shall review the need for this sub-paragraph not later than 30 June 1960.

(italics in the original)

The GATT/WTO case law has clarified a number of points relating to the understanding of this provision. First, the WTO Member invoking Art. XX GATT has the *burden of proof* – it must demonstrate that its policies can be justified through recourse to this provision. The term *burden of proof* can be further distinguished in *burden of production*, and *burden of persuasion*, the latter usually captured by the term *standard of review.* The burden of persuasion varies across the various sub-paragraphs included in Art. XX GATT. Second, the list in Art. XX is exhaustive. In the GATT context, there is nothing like a "political exception" justifying deviations. Third, only the *means* used by WTO Members are justiciable. The *ends* sought cannot be put into question by WTO adjudicating bodies. For example, if a WTO Member invokes Art. XX(b) GATT to protect the life of an animal, a WTO panel or the AB cannot dismiss such invocation on the grounds that the animal at hand is not an endangered species. This proposition is the natural outcome of the negative integration sought through the GATT. As a result, a WTO adjudicating body cannot simply be equated to that of a domestic/federal judge.

Fourth, conformity of an otherwise GATT-inconsistent measure must be established by using any one of the sub-paragraphs of Art. XX GATT as benchmark. The legal standard for compliance is not the same in each and every sub-paragraph of Art. XX GATT, for example, whereas sub-paragraph (b) requires that measures used are necessary (in the sense, not more trade restrictive than what is required to achieve the stated objective)[28] to reach a goal, sub-paragraph (h) requires that measures are simply relating to the attainment of the objective (a substantially less demanding standard, equivalent more or less to an appropriateness test, i.e., is a particular measure appropriate to reach a certain goal independently whether it is the least restrictive option?).

Once substantial conformity has been satisfied, WTO Members must ensure that they apply their measure in a manner consistent with the *chapeau* of Art. XX GATT. Hence, there is a dichotomy between sub-paragraphs and the *chapeau* in the sense that the former are relevant as far as substantial conformity is concerned whereas the latter are relevant only as far as the application of an otherwise WTO-consistent measure is concerned. The *chapeau* has been interpreted as more or less requiring WTO Members to apply their measures in an even-handed manner among constituencies where the same conditions prevail.

The GATT *US – Tuna (Mexico)* panel report in 1989 outlawed a US measure aimed at protecting dolphins because it was unilateral and, in its view, only WTO-wide bargaining solutions are WTO-consistent; absent such solutions, transaction costs are much higher as a result of the pursuance of unilateral policies. Wrong, because unilateral, is a brief way to describe this report. In its report on *US – Shrimp*, the AB reversed this kind of thinking. Without pronouncing clearly on what is public international law-conforming exercise of jurisdiction, it accepted as in principle legitimate a US regulatory intervention whereby the US imposes on both domestic and foreign fishermen of shrimps a fishing technique that is aimed at ensuring that sea turtles will not be accidentally killed. We quote from § 133 of the report:

> We do not pass upon the question of whether there is an implied jurisdictional limitation in Article XX(g), and if so, the nature or extent of that limitation. We note only that in the specific circumstances of the case before us, there is a sufficient nexus between the migratory and endangered marine populations involved and the United States for purposes of Article XX(g).

This is probably the single most spectacular reversal of GATT case law. The implication is that absent explicit transfer of sovereignty, WTO Members are free to pursue policies as long they are non-discriminatory. However, there is a logical inconsistency in the manner in which WTO adjudicating bodies have dealt with the relationship between Art. III and Art. XX GATT. As both provisions require non-discriminatory behavior, one cannot be an exception to the other. Assume a WTO Member pursues an objective that is not included in the exhaustive Art. XX list and uses a measure that violates Art. III GATT (national treatment). The country will find it difficult to justify its measures through Art. XX as it is pursuing an objective that it should not be pursuing. Such an interpretation of Art. XX would imply the GATT is an instrument for *de-regulation* rather than *non-discrimination*. This is not its agreed objective function. Assume now a WTO Member pursues an objective which is included in Art. XX but again violates Art. III. It will again have a hard time to justify its measures under Art. XX since it will be asked to demonstrate that a discriminatory measure has somehow been transformed into a non-discriminatory one. For these reasons, Art. XX GATT arguably should be viewed as a general exception to all GATT provisions *except* Art. III GATT. The implication is that higher evidentiary standards should be required for complainants challenging the consistency of a measure with Art. III.

National security

Art. XXI GATT allows WTO Members to adopt trade restrictions that are inconsistent with their WTO obligations if necessary to protect their national security.[29] Few invocations of Art. XXI GATT have been challenged before a panel. The only case that went all the way to a GATT panel was a dispute between Nicaragua and the United States. This led to a report that was never adopted, and hence is of limited legal value (*US – Sugar Quota*). What is important to note in this respect is the standard of review applied in such cases. The question whether the term "necessary" appearing in Art. XXI GATT should be of secondary importance since it is predicated on the applicable overall standard of review. To date, the only panel report and the ensuing discussions in the GATT Council have opted for a deferential standard of review when dealing with national security cases.[30] This should not come as a surprise: a similar standard of review is applied to the same category of cases in substantially more integrated schemes like the European Community.[31] There is of course a trade-off in the sense that a deferential standard might theoretically invite abuses, but to date, such fears have proven unfounded.

Institutional

There is a final category of state contingencies[32] where the motivation is more systemic – to allow Members to pursue actions that are inconsistent with the core rules because the majority of the membership perceives this to be in the interest of the trading system. The main examples are regional integration (free trade areas and customs unions), and special and differential treatment of developing countries and waivers.

Reciprocal preferential trade agreements (PTAs)

Article XXIV GATT permits the formation of free trade agreements and customs unions. The rationale for this exception is that countries should be allowed to engage in far-reaching integration initiatives of the type that may ultimately lead to the creation of new political entities – as was the case with the nineteenth-century *Zollverein*, which was a stepping stone to the eventual creation of a federal German state. The formation of a PTA is subject to conditions. Thus:

1 External trade barriers after integration may not rise on average (Art. XXIV.5 GATT).
2 All tariffs and other regulations of commerce must be removed on substantially all intra-regional exchanges of goods within a reasonable length of time (Art. XXIV.8 GATT).
3 PTAs must be notified to the WTO (Art. XXIV.7 GATT).

It is for the WTO Council for Trade in Goods to determine, on the basis of a recommendation of the Committee on Regional Trade Agreements (CRTA) whether the criteria reflected in Art. XXIV GATT are satisfied. Under the GATT 1947 there was effectively no enforcement of Art. XXIV. Starting with the examination of the Treaty of Rome establishing the European Economic Community in 1957, virtually no examination of notified PTAs led to a unanimous conclusion regarding their conformity with the legal GATT requirements. The initial reason for this was a fear that a finding that the EEC violated Art. XXIV because of the exclusion of agriculture from the free trade provisions could have induced the six European countries to leave the GATT. This created a precedent, with the result that there is now a huge "overhang" of agreements that have never been approved. In addition to this political factor, a complementary reason for this is that the language of GATT Article XXIV is ambiguous. Legitimate differences of opinion can exist regarding how to define "substantially all trade," how to determine whether the external trade policy of a customs union has become more restrictive on average, and what is a reasonable length of time for the transition towards full implementation of an agreement.

Compared to the GATT 1947, the WTO clarifies some of the criteria and procedures for the assessment of agreements. There is a 10-year maximum for the transition period for implementation of an agreement, although allowance is made for exceptional circumstances. The evaluation of the general incidence of the duties and other regulations of commerce applicable before and after the formation of a customs union is to be based upon "an overall assessment of weighted average tariff rates and of customs duties collected" by the WTO Secretariat, based on import statistics for a previous representative period on a tariff line basis, broken down by WTO Member country of origin. The definition of the term *substantially all trade* appearing in Art. XXIV.8 GATT, on the other hand, has not been clarified in WTO practice.[33] In part, this may be because there should be less of an incentive to do so: except for complementary products, non-members are better off if they face a less integrated PTA as there will be less trade diversion.

To satisfy the external trade policy requirement, a customs union must ensure consistency with Art. XXIV.5 GATT and Art. XXIV.6 GATT. The latter requires WTO members seeking to increase bound tariff rates upon joining a customs union to enter into re-negotiations under Art. XXVIII GATT on compensatory adjustment by offering to reduce duties on other tariff lines, or to otherwise provide compensation. If agreement cannot be reached within a reasonable period, the customs union may proceed as it wishes and affected members may withdraw equivalent concessions (retaliate).

When the WTO was established in 1995, all but three of the original 120 Members were parties to at least one of the 62 PTAs still in force at that time, the exceptions being Japan, Hong Kong and Korea.[34] Two of these countries, Japan and South Korea, have now also negotiated PTAs. Virtually all countries that acceded to the WTO after 1995 are also members of PTAs. A total of some 350 PTAs are now believed to be in place, 200 of which have been notified to the WTO. The proliferation of PTAs is paradoxical, given that the substantial reduction of tariffs at the multilateral level that has taken place over time should reduce the incentives for going regional: how can it be that countries simultaneously pursue the *global* and the *preferential* perspective?[35]

One explanation for the plethora of PTAs is that they are not pursued solely for commercial (trade) purposes. PTAs may offer a stronger "lock-in" mechanism for policy reform than the WTO, insofar as the partners involved have stronger incentives to enforce agreements. They may also involve disciplines on domestic instruments that are not (yet) covered by the WTO, providing a laboratory for countries to explore mechanisms of cooperation on "behind the border" policies with similar or like-minded partners.

Economists have tended to view PTAs with skepticism, noting that they may divert trade away from the most efficient suppliers in the world to more costly, but preferred, partners, who are able to sell more in the PTA because they are exempted from duties. This is not to say that PTAs necessarily reduce welfare. They may create more trade than they divert, by inducing consumers to switch from less efficient local producers to firms in partner countries that are more efficient. However, PTAs that are beneficial to members may still have negative impacts on those countries that suffer trade diversion.

An important systemic question is thus, whether PTAs slow down multilateral liberalization. This is an empirical issue, and one that is difficult to answer as it is very difficult to determine what the counterfactual should be. PTAs could be building blocks for multilateral liberalization if their formation induces excluded countries to pursue WTO negotiations to lower the external tariffs of the PTAs so as to reduce trade-diverting potential. It has often been argued that the formation of the EC and its periodic expansion were one motivation for GATT rounds of negotiations. Recent research has offered some evidence that PTAs may be stumbling blocks: both the US and the EU offer fewer concessions multilaterally on products that are of interest to their PTA partners.[36]

The legal test enshrined in Art. XXIV GATT and Art. V GATS does not enquire into the motives of countries entering into PTAs or the welfare implications of specific PTAs. It simply aims to make departures from MFN onerous. The CRTA is the first track (Track I) to review consistency of PTAs. It is composed of all WTO representatives and decisions are taken by consensus. This means that the WTO Members participating in a PTA must be persuaded that their PTA is WTO-inconsistent for a decision to this effect to be taken. Not surprisingly, this has never happened. There have been only a handful of instances where PTAs were judged *broadly* consistent with the GATT. Since the formation of the WTO there has been one case where there has been one definitive and unambiguous acceptance, at the CRTA level, that a notified PTA was GATT-consistent: the customs union between the Czech and the Slovak republics. Thus, for the remaining 99 percent of all PTAs currently in place, it is unknown whether they are consistent with the WTO rules.

This raises the question whether non-members of a PTA can seek to contest a CRTA review before a WTO panel (Track II), arguing that Art. I GATT has been violated and/or that specific provisions of a PTA violate Art. XXIV GATT. The WTO Understanding on Art. XXIV GATT (adopted during the Uruguay Round) states that the DSU may be invoked with respect to *any* matter arising from the application of the provisions of Article XXIV relating to customs unions, free-trade areas or interim agreements leading to the formation of a customs union or a free-trade area. While one can question whether WTO panels are well equipped to deal with such complicated issues, both in terms of expertise and the time constraints under which they must operate, a comprehensive review of a PTA by panels is not unthinkable.

An important matter is whether panels should stop short of deciding whether a PTA is WTO-consistent in cases where the Committee on Regional Trade Agreements (CRTA) has not pronounced on its consistency. This would arguably not be appropriate. If panels were to behave in this way, they would risk depriving WTO Members of their MFN rights: the CRTA will invariably take a long time to reach consensus, and, as practice shows, the consensus will, in all likelihood, reflect an agreement to disagree. On the other hand, the CRTA should not be bound by a panel (or Appellate Body) decision on the consistency of a PTA with the relevant WTO rules.

WTO Members have rarely challenged the consistency of a PTA before a panel, even though the burden on complainants is relatively low. WTO Members often seem to lack the incentives to contest the validity of PTAs, reflecting either the fact that virtually all WTO members are engaged in PTAs (the "glass house" syndrome) and/or that, their competence notwithstanding, panels lack the necessary prerequisites to pronounce on such a complicated issue.

Special and differential treatment of developing countries

Reflecting a common perception that many developing countries would not benefit from trade liberalization or from the implementation of some of the core principles of the GATT, and that higher income countries should provide preferential access to their markets to goods produced in developing countries, a variety of provisions are included in the GATT that provide for differential and more favorable treatment for such countries.[37] As the natural outcome of the MFN obligation is a "level playing field," any differential treatment for a subset of the membership requires discrimination. The legal space for providing discriminatory, more favorable treatment of developing countries was created through the 1979 (Tokyo Round) Decision on Differential and More Favorable Treatment of Developing Countries (the so-called Enabling Clause). This provides the legal cover for the Generalized System of Preferences (GSP), as well as specific exceptions (exemptions) from GATT rules for developing countries. Thus, for example, developing countries are only expected to offer reciprocal concessions in trade negotiations that are consistent with their development needs, they may, if they wish, establish trade agreements that do not meet the conditions of Article XXIV.

What constitutes a developing country is not defined in the WTO. It is left to the so-called "self-election" principle. That is, in application of the public international law principle of sovereignty, WTO Members can self-elect if they qualify as developing countries.[38] However, there are specific sub-sets of developing countries that are formally defined in WTO agreements. Examples are the least-developed country (LDC) group – a UN-defined set of countries – net food importing developing countries, and countries with a per capita income level below $1,000 (used to define eligibility to use export subsidies under the SCM Agreement). A recent addition are countries that do not have a domestic pharmaceutical industry in the context of the Declaration on TRIPs and Public Health (see below).

Waivers

The waiver procedure is designed to legitimize temporary deviations from the WTO contract by a country or group of countries when the

WTO membership regards this to be in the interest of the institution. An important example was a waiver granted to the EU for its preferences for African, Caribbean and Pacific (ACP) countries. The waiver procedure was carried over from the GATT into the WTO. The relevant provision (Art. IX.3 and 4 WTO) reads:

3   In exceptional circumstances, the Ministerial Conference may decide to waive an obligation imposed on a Member by this Agreement or any of the Multilateral Trade Agreements, provided that any such decision shall be taken by three fourths[39] of the Members unless otherwise provided for in this paragraph.

  (a) A request for a waiver concerning this Agreement shall be submitted to the Ministerial Conference for consideration pursuant to the practice of decision-making by consensus. The Ministerial Conference shall establish a time-period, which shall not exceed 90 days, to consider the request. If consensus is not reached during the time-period, any decision to grant a waiver shall be taken by three fourths of the Members.

  (b) A request for a waiver concerning the Multilateral Trade Agreements [GATT, GATS, TRIPS] ... shall be submitted initially to the [relevant] Council ... for consideration during a time-period which shall not exceed 90 days. At the end of the time-period, the relevant Council shall submit a report to the Ministerial Conference.

4   A decision by the Ministerial Conference granting a waiver shall state the exceptional circumstances justifying the decision, the terms and conditions governing the application of the waiver, and the date on which the waiver shall terminate. Any waiver granted for a period of more than one year shall be reviewed by the Ministerial Conference not later than one year after it is granted, and thereafter annually until the waiver terminates. In each review, the Ministerial Conference shall examine whether the exceptional circumstances justifying the waiver still exist and whether the terms and conditions attached to the waiver have been met. The Ministerial Conference, on the basis of the annual review, may extend, modify or terminate the waiver.

Note that in principle even an obligation such as the MFN rule can be waived.

4   Services and intellectual property

There were no multilateral disciplines on trade in services or most intellectual property rights prior to the advent of the WTO – the addition of rules in these areas was one of the innovations of the Uruguay Round. The relevant disciplines are contained in the General Agreement on Trade in Services (GATS) and the Agreement on Trade-related Aspects of Intellectual Property Rights (TRIPs), respectively.

The GATS

The GATS is divided into general obligations (applicable to all services sectors – MFN being the major example) and specific commitments that bind WTO Members on a sectoral basis to provide national treatment and market access, subject to possible scheduled exceptions. The reason for this bifurcation is that customs duties or QRs enforced at the border are often not feasible instruments to affect trade, given the intangible nature of services. Most obstacles to international trade take the form of domestic regulation, including recognition of qualifications, constraints on operations or equity ownership, etc. The main substantive provisions of the GATS are summarized in Box 4.1.

Box 4.1 Major provisions of the GATS

I   Trade in services is defined to cover four modes of supply.
II   MFN obligation. Option to invoke exemptions on a one-time basis.
III   Notification and publication. Obligation to create an enquiry point.

IV	Developed countries to take measures to facilitate trade of developing nations.
V	Allows for economic integration agreements between members.
VI	Domestic regulation. Requirements concerning the design and implementation of service sector regulation, including in particular qualification requirements.
VII	Recognition of qualifications, standards and certification of suppliers.
VIII	Requires that monopolies and exclusive suppliers abide by MFN, specific commitments (Articles XVI and XVII) and do not abuse a dominant position.
IX	Recognition that business practices may restrict trade. Call for consultations between Members on request.
XIV	General exceptions. Allows measures to achieve non-economic objectives.
XVI	Market access. Defines a set of policies that may only be used to restrict market access for a scheduled sector if they are listed in a Member's specific commitments.
XVII	National treatment. Applies in a sector if a commitment to that effect is made and no limitations or exceptions are listed in a Member's schedule.
XVIII	Additional commitments. Catch-all provision allowing Members to list additional commitments in their schedules. Used in case of telecommunications for Members to commit to the so-called "Reference Paper."
XIX	Calls for successive negotiations to expand coverage of specific commitments.

The GATS covers not only cross-border trade, but also transactions that involve the cross-border movement of service suppliers, as well as the temporary movement of service consumers. As binding commitments across these "modes of supply" would have implied very far-reaching liberalization, negotiators decided to opt for an agreement that is characterized by much greater flexibility than the GATT. The extent of liberalization of services trade depends importantly on the content of sector-specific commitments. This contrasts with the GATT where national treatment is a general commitment. Under the GATS, national treatment is a specific commitment; MFN, by contrast, is a general obligation.

To date, the GATS has not generated much in the way of actual liberalization – instead negotiating efforts largely revolve around locking in prior unilateral liberalization efforts. The GATS, though, offers a basis for future negotiations to open up services trade further.

General obligations

The subject matter of the general obligations imposed by the GATS on all WTO Members include the MFN obligation (Art. II), transparency (Art. III), an obligation to negotiate aspects of domestic regulation (Art. VI), and some rather superficial competition-related commitments (Arts. VIII and IX). In contrast to the GATT, the GATS allowed for *political* exceptions from the MFN obligation, provided that these were scheduled at the entry into force of the WTO. Thus, a Member can indicate the countries to which it does not wish to grant MFN status. The Annex on Art. II states that in principle such exceptions should not last for more than ten years.

The general obligations of the GATS are all rather weak. One possible exception is Art. VI GATS which calls for WTO Members to establish an independent forum to judge in an impartial manner the impacts of regulation on trade in services. It also requires that measures relating to qualification requirements and procedures, technical standards and licensing requirements "do not constitute unnecessary barriers to trade in services." To date, the only relevant work in this field has been undertaken in the context of professional services and, more specifically, in the accountancy sector. A Working Party was established which prepared non-binding guidelines for mutual recognition of accountancy qualifications. These were adopted by the CTS in a document laying out the obligations of WTO Members in the accountancy sector, even if no specific commitments have been undertaken (WTO Doc. S/L/64 of 17 December 1998). In 1999, a Working Party on Domestic Regulation was established with the mandate to develop any necessary disciplines to ensure that measures relating to licensing requirements and procedures, technical standards and qualification requirements and procedures do not constitute unnecessary barriers to trade in services.

Modes of supply

Reflecting the characteristics of services that make them inherently less tradable than goods, Art. I.2 GATS defines trade in services as spanning four modes of supply (Table 4.1).

- Neither the service supplier nor the service consumer has to move (an attorney in country A sends by fax expertise to a company in country B) – *Mode 1*.
- The consumer moves to the country where the service is supplied (a consumer from country B travels to his/her attorney in country A where he/she procures an attorney service) – *Mode 2*.
- The service supplier establishes *commercial presence* in the country where he/she supplies the service (an attorney from country A establishes a *law firm* in country B) –*Mode 3*.
- A service supplier (a natural person in this case and not a legal person like in *Mode 3*) is established in a different country (an attorney from country A represents a client before a court in country B) – *Mode 4*.

Mode 3 essentially amounts to an international agreement to liberalize investment: by allowing, for example, foreign banks (or foreign insurance companies, etc.) to sell banking services under Mode 3, a WTO Member is *de facto* opening up to foreign investment in the banking sector.

The literature often refers to Mode 4 as the means to liberalize temporary (and not permanent) presence of natural persons. The only indication to this effect is contextual and reflected in the Annex on

Table 4.1 Modes of supply

Supplier presence	Other criteria	Mode
Service supplier *not present* within the territory of the Member	Service delivered within the territory of the Member, from the territory of another Member	CROSS-BORDER SUPPLY
	Service delivered outside the territory of the Member, i.e., outside the consumer's territory	CONSUMPTION ABROAD
Service supplier *present* within the territory of the Member	Service delivered within the territory of the Member, through the commercial presence of the supplier	COMMERCIAL PRESENCE
	Service delivered within the territory of the Member, with supplier present as a natural person	PRESENCE OF NATURAL PERSON

Source: WTO Doc. S/L/92.198

movement of natural persons supplying services under the agreement. In § 4, the Annex reads:

> The Agreement shall not prevent a Member from applying measures to regulate the entry of natural persons into, or their *temporary stay* in, its territory, including those measures necessary to protect the integrity of, and to ensure the orderly movement of natural persons across, its borders, provided that such measures are not applied in such a manner as to nullify or impair the benefits accruing to any Member under the terms of a specific commitment.
>
> (emphasis added)

However, nothing stops a WTO Member from entering into long-term commitments under *Mode 4*.

Specific commitments

Specific commitments are the core of the GATS – the analogue to tariff bindings under the GATT. The structure of commitments made by WTO Members on services is complex, taking the form of a positive listing of sectors that are subject to market access and national treatment obligations, in each case being defined negatively: a commitment exists to provide market access and national treatment for a sector and a specific mode of supply only if no exceptions are scheduled.

The classification of services is largely based on the United Nations Central Product Classification (CPC), which uses a numerical method that is analogous to the HS for goods, to define services sectors. The schedule of each WTO Member comprises four columns reflecting the mode of supply and the three GATS Articles which govern specific commitments (Table 4.2).

A Member has three broad choices: it may schedule "*None*," meaning that it does not impose any limitation on the cross-border supply of legal advice to its sovereignty;[1] "*Unbound*," implying it is essentially free to regulate as it deems appropriate (no commitment of any kind has been made); or it may introduce *specific language* to describe its commitment. According to the terminology used in the *2001 Scheduling Guidelines*, the first category of this specific language is known as *full commitment* (§§ 42 and 43); the second, *no commitment* (§ 46); and the third, *commitment with limitations* (§§ 44 and 45). The *2001 Scheduling Guidelines*[2] contain two more levels of commitments: *no commitment technically feasible* (§ 47), and *special cases* (§§ 48 and 49).[3]

Table 4.2 Structure and example of a GATS schedule of specific commitments

Mode of supply	Conditions and limitations on market access	Conditions and qualifications on national treatment	Additional commitments
1 Cross-border	Commercial presence required	Unbound	
2 Consumption abroad	None	None	
3 Commercial presence (FDI)	25% of management to be nationals	Unbound	Establishment of an independent regulator
4 Temporary entry of natural persons	Unbound, except as indicated in Horizontal Commitments	Unbound, except as indicated in Horizontal Commitments	

Notes:
"None" implies no exceptions are maintained – that is, a bound commitment not to apply any measures that are inconsistent with market access or national treatment. "Unbound" implies no commitment of any kind has been made.

The first column of a schedule pertains to Art. XVI GATS (market access). This lays out six measures restricting market access. In principle, WTO Members do not have recourse to any of these measures, unless they state that they maintain such measures in their schedule, or state that they wish to retain the freedom to do so. Restrictions can be lawfully entered with respect to one, several or all four modes of supply. In sectors where market-access commitments are undertaken, the measures which a Member may not maintain unless otherwise specified in its Schedule, are defined as:

1   limitations on the number of service suppliers whether in the form of numerical quotas, monopolies, exclusive service suppliers or the requirements of an economic needs test;
2   limitations on the total value of service transactions or assets in the form of numerical quotas or the requirement of an economic needs test;
3   limitations on the total number of service operations or on the total quantity of service output expressed in terms of designated numerical units in the form of quotas or the requirement of an economic needs test;[4]

4 limitations on the total number of natural persons that may be employed in a particular service sector or that a service supplier may employ and who are necessary for, and directly related to, the supply of a specific service in the form of numerical quotas or the requirement of an economic needs test;

5 measures which restrict or require specific types of legal entity or joint venture through which a service supplier may supply a service; and

6 limitations on the participation of foreign capital in terms of maximum percentage limit on foreign shareholding or the total value of individual or aggregate foreign investment.

The second column of each schedule relates to Art. XVII GATS: national treatment. WTO Members, are free to deviate from national treatment and provide foreign suppliers treatment inferior to that provided to national suppliers of the like service (§1, Art. XVII GATS): complete freedom to restrict national treatment may be retained by writing "unbound" into a cell, see Table 4.2. Only if a member writes "none" in all the cells of its schedule for a sector is there a binding commitment not to restrict market access and to abide by national treatment.

The third column of each schedule relates to Art. XVIII GATS, which allows for "additional commitments." So far, this possibility has been used comprehensively in the case of telecommunications. The Agreement on Basic Telecommunications includes a "Reference Paper," which was deemed necessary in order to ensure that interconnection services be provided on a cost basis.[5]

For a complete picture of sectoral commitments, it is also necessary to consider the so-called "horizontal commitments" – generally applicable provisions and restrictions that apply to all modes of supply, as well as the list of MFN exemptions that each WTO Member has deposited with the WTO.

The relationship between national treatment and market access

Whether the limitations of Art. XVI GATS are relevant for foreign suppliers only or for foreign *and* domestic suppliers; and whether national treatment applies to any Art. XVI GATS restriction, are questions that are somewhat ambiguous. The *US – Gambling* panel found (and the AB concurred) that a series of US federal and state measures which regulate the supply of services by foreign and domestic suppliers alike, violated Art. XVI GATS. Two examples of such laws were the *Federal Wire Act* and the *Illegal Gambling Act* (*IGBA*). The first reads in part:

> Whoever being engaged in the business of betting or wagering knowingly uses a wire communication facility for the transmission in interstate or foreign commerce of bets and wagers or information assisting in the placing of bets or wagers or any sporting event or contest, or for the transmission of a wire communication which entitles the recipient to receive money or credit as a result of bets or wagers shall be fined under this title or imprisoned not more than two years, or both.

The *IGBA* states that "Whoever conducts, finances, manages, supervises, directs or owns all or part of an illegal gambling business shall be fined under this title or imprisoned not more than five years, or both."

We believe that this approach is wrong both from a legal and from a policy (trade liberalization) perspective. The GATS is a trade agreement; it should not regulate the conditions of access to a market for the citizens of a state making a liberalization commitment. All that is required is that the measure be transparent. To this effect, Art. III GATS obliges WTO Members to "publish promptly ... all relevant measures of general application which pertain to or affect the operation of this Agreement." This provision arguably leaves some discretion to the regulating state as to what is covered under this transparency obligation. In the worst case scenario, a dispute may be initiated. It is also possible for a WTO Member to cross-notify (under Art. III.5 GATS): laws of general application, even if not notified to the WTO, will become public because of domestic law constraints.

From a policy perspective, it seems that trade liberalization will indeed be served were one to restrict the applicability of Art. XVI GATS to foreign services and services suppliers only: the limitations indicated in a schedule of concessions will be at the mercy of foreigners only (who will not have to compete with domestic suppliers for that part of the market).

Since the GATS involves scheduling of domestic regulations, it seems plausible to view Art. XVI as a sub-set of Art. XVII. The implication is that WTO Members must first decide whether or not to accord national treatment to foreign services and services suppliers. If so, they will have to indicate this in the column for Art. XVII GATS (to comply with Art. III on transparency). If not, the same reporting requirement obtains. Assuming a government decides not to accord national treatment, and that it wants the relatively more onerous market access to be expressed in Art. XVI GATS terms, it will choose an instrument reflected in Art. XVI.2 GATS. This will have to indicate their concession (which should be termed *limitation* or *restriction*) under the column "Art. XVI GATS."[6] This construction of Art. XVI GATS, in our view, best serves the objective function of this provision. It should be stressed that it does not, however, coincide with the understanding of Art. XVI GATS by WTO adjudicating bodies.[7]

Remaining provisions

As is the case under GATT, the GATS allows for re-negotiation of schedules (Art. XXI GATS), and contains balance of payments, public order and national security exceptions (Arts. XII, XIV and XIV *bis*). In contrast to the GATT, it does not contain any provisions relating to subsidies, contingent protection (safeguards) or government procurement. Little progress was achieved by the Working Group on GATS Rules on these subjects. Procurement of services is, however, covered by the Government Procurement Agreement for signatories to that agreement (see Chapter 5). The absence of safeguards is arguably not a problem in light of the flexibility that exists in scheduling liberalization in the GATS. Indeed, a distinguishing feature of the GATS is the high degree of flexibility members enjoy in terms of the depth and coverage of commitments. This also explains why, in contrast to the GATT, there are virtually no special and differential treatment provisions for developing countries – these were not needed.

The TRIPs Agreement

The Agreement on Trade-Related Aspects of Intellectual Property Rights (TRIPs) is the third multilateral agreement contained in the WTO. Negotiated in the Uruguay Round, TRIPs essentially reproduces the critical aspects of four international agreements in the field of intellectual property. The four agreements are:

1 the *Paris Convention* (1967) for the protection of industrial property;
2 the *Berne Convention* (1971) for the protection of copyright;
3 the *Rome Convention* (1961) for the protection of performers, producers of phonograms and broadcasting organizations;
4 the *IPIC* (integrated circuits) treaty (1989).

The TRIPs Agreement essentially multilateralized the main provisions of these treaties to the extent of their incorporation in the Agreement.[8]

Developing country members were granted transitional periods – for non-LDCs, these expired on 31 December 1999. For least developed countries transition periods initially ran through 1 January 2006, with a longer period with respect to product patent protection of pharmaceutical products (until 2016).

TRIPs imposes *minimum standards* with respect to the protection of intellectual property rights: WTO Members must, at the very least, comply with the obligations laid down in the agreement but retain the discretion to adopt higher standards of protection (Art. 1 TRIPs). Subject to certain exceptions laid down in Art. 3 TRIPs, WTO Members must grant national treatment to IPR holders. Note that in contrast to both the GATT and the GATS, what is implied by TRIPs is positive integration, i.e., harmonization of regulatory standards, and not the removal of barriers to trade. Rights are protected on a territorial basis which means that IPR owners are entitled to request protection in the territory of the WTO Members of interest to them (where protection will be sought and is thus not a function of a cost-benefit calculus by the inventor or owner of the knowledge).

The intellectual property rights covered

The rights protected under the TRIPs Agreement include copyright, trademarks, industrial designs, integrated circuit designs, patents, geographical indications, and undisclosed information:[9]

1 *Copyright and related rights.* Art. 9.2 TRIPs requires that copyright protection extend to expressions and not to ideas, procedures, methods of operation or mathematical concepts as such. The rights protected include computer programs, cinematographic films, databases, performers, producers of phonograms and broadcasting organizations. The protection granted is for the life of the natural person and can extend at least for 50 years from the end of the calendar year of authorized publication (Art. 12 TRIPs) and 20 years for broadcasting organizations (Art. 14.5 TRIPs).
2 *Trademarks and industrial designs.* Art. 15 TRIPs defines these as any sign, or any combination of signs, capable of distinguishing the goods or services of one undertaking from those of other undertakings. Such signs shall be eligible for registration as trademarks. Where signs are not inherently capable of distinguishing the relevant goods or services, Members may make registrability depend on distinctiveness acquired through use. Members may require, as a condition of registration, that signs be visually perceptible. Actual

use of a trademark may not be a condition for filing an application for registration. Members must publish each trademark either before it is registered or promptly after it is registered and shall afford a reasonable opportunity for petitions to cancel the registration. The initial registration of trademarks is for at least seven years and their registration can be renewed indefinitely (Art. 18 TRIPs). Art. 25 TRIPs requires WTO Members to protect independently created, new and original industrial designs. Protection of industrial designs runs for at least 10 years.

3 *Geographical indications.* Arts. 22 and 23 TRIPs govern the protection of such rights. Art. 23 TRIPs makes it clear in its title that the protection conferred to wines and spirits is *additional* to that conferred to other goods under Art. 22 TRIPs. One basic rationale for this protection has to do with consumer protection (avoid misleading consumers through deceptive use of geographical indications). Protection of geographical indications knows many exceptions (Art. 24 TRIPs), such as, for example, the possibility to stop protecting an indication which has become a generic term for describing a particular product.

4 *Patents.* Art. 27.1 TRIPs requires patents be available for any inventions, whether products or processes, in all fields of technology, provided that they are new, involve an inventive step and are capable of industrial application.[10] Subject to Art. 65:4, Art. 70:8, and Art. 27:3, patents are to be available and patent rights enjoyable without discrimination as to the place of invention, the field of technology and whether products are imported or locally produced. Hence, not only products but also processes used to obtain a product can be patented.

Art. 27:2 and Art. 27:3 TRIPs provide for the possibility to exclude some specific inventions from the scope of *patentability.* No specific inventions are excluded. Instead, the Articles establish criteria which if met, can be used to deny patent protection. The three exceptions concern public health, morals, etc. – unilaterally defined to reflect national preferences – specific therapeutic and/or surgical methods for the treatment of human beings or animals; and plants and animals other than micro-organisms, and essentially biological processes for the production of plants or animals other than non-biological and microbiological processes (Art. 27.3(b) TRIPs). Members must, however, provide for the protection of plant varieties either by patents or by an effective *sui generis* system or by any combination thereof. The latter provisions were to be reviewed four years after the date of entry into force of the WTO Agreement.

The rights conferred to patents are laid out in Art. 28 TRIPs:

1   A patent shall confer on its owner the following exclusive rights:
   i   where the subject matter of a patent is a product, to prevent third parties not having the owner's consent from the acts of: making, using, offering for sale, selling, or importing[11] for these purposes that product;
   ii where the subject matter of a patent is a process, to prevent third parties not having the owner's consent from the act of using the process, and from the acts of: using, offering for sale, selling, or importing for these purposes at least the product obtained directly by that process.
2   Patent owners shall also have the right to assign, or transfer by succession, the patent and to conclude licensing contracts.

WTO Members can restrict the exclusive rights conferred to patents, provided that such restrictions do not unreasonably conflict with a normal exploitation of the patent at hand (Art. 30 TRIPs). The length of patent protection is at least 20 years counting from the filing date (Art. 33 TRIPs). Patents can be "broken" through compulsory licensing: Art. 31 TRIPs lays out in some detail the conditions for a compulsory licensing requirement to be WTO-consistent, including adequate compensation.

International exhaustion of intellectual property rights

The TRIPs Agreement leaves open the issue of exhaustion of IP rights. For example, under EC law, a German IPR owner who sells its goods to a German wholesaler has "exhausted" its IP right. That is, if the wholesaler re-sells the goods to a Dutch trader who re-exports them to Germany, the IP owner does not have the legal right to block the parallel imports. If the German wholesaler sells to the US and the goods are then re-exported to Europe, matters are less clear. TRIPS Art. 6 allows for regulatory diversity in this respect. WTO Members are free to decide how to define international exhaustion.

The TRIPs Agreement and developing countries

Developing country WTO Members have expressed concerns about a number of aspects of the TRIPs Agreement. One of their concerns relates to the potential problems of countries without domestic production capacity to use the compulsory licensing provisions of TRIPS

(Art. 31) in case of a public health need. After contentious negotiations this matter was addressed through a decision of 30 August 2003, to permit LDCs and countries without local pharmaceutical production capacity to import drugs from other WTO Members on the basis of a compulsory license issued by the importer to the exporting firms. Preconditions are that the eligible importing Members notify the Council for TRIPS, and specify the names and expected quantities of the product(s) needed. If a non-LDC confirms that it has insufficient or no manufacturing capacities in the pharmaceutical sector and confirms that, where a pharmaceutical product is patented in its territory, it has granted or intends to grant a compulsory license in accordance with Article 31 TRIPS and the provisions of the Decision, the license issued by the exporting Member should be limited to what is needed to address the public health requirements of the importing country. Products also should be clearly identified as being produced under the system set out in the Decision through specific labeling and special packaging.

Adequate remuneration is to be paid to license holders, and LDCs are to monitor use and take action to prevent re-exportation (if needed, technical assistance to ensure this may be requested), are encouraged to use the system to promote the development of a local industrial capacity, and all WTO Members are to ensure that parallel imports of the products can be prevented. In December 2005, the General Council adopted a Protocol amending the TRIPS Agreement to incorporate this Decision. In substance, the amendment closely tracks the August 2003 text. The Protocol will enter into force upon acceptance by two-thirds of the Members. In the meantime, the waiver provisions of the August 2003 Decision remain applicable until the date on which the amendment takes effect for a Member.

Enforcement of intellectual property rights

The TRIPs Agreement requires WTO Members to adopt fair and equitable procedures to ensure adequate protection of IP rights in their sovereignty. Besides the general obligations, the Agreement provides provisional measures and criminal procedures if needed. Art. 41 TRIPs lays out the general obligations of WTO Members:

1 Members shall ensure that enforcement procedures as specified in this Part are available under their law so as to permit effective action against any act of infringement of intellectual property rights covered by this Agreement, including expeditious remedies

to prevent infringements and remedies which constitute a deterrent to further infringements. These procedures shall be applied in such a manner as to avoid the creation of barriers to legitimate trade and to provide for safeguards against their abuse.

2   Procedures concerning the enforcement of intellectual property rights shall be fair and equitable. They shall not be unnecessarily complicated or costly, or entail unreasonable time-limits or unwarranted delays.

3   Decisions on the merits of a case shall preferably be in writing and reasoned. They shall be made available at least to the parties to the proceeding without undue delay. Decisions on the merits of a case shall be based only on evidence in respect of which parties were offered the opportunity to be heard.

4   Parties to a proceeding shall have an opportunity for review by a judicial authority of final administrative decisions and, subject to jurisdictional provisions in a Member's law concerning the importance of a case, of at least the legal aspects of initial judicial decisions on the merits of a case. However, there shall be no obligation to provide an opportunity for review of acquittals in criminal cases.

5   It is understood that this Part does not create any obligation to put in place a judicial system for the enforcement of intellectual property rights distinct from that for the enforcement of law in general, nor does it affect the capacity of Members to enforce their law in general. Nothing in this Part creates any obligation with respect to the distribution of resources as between enforcement of intellectual property rights and the enforcement of law in general.

Enforcement of IP rights is costly. According to WTO case law, WTO Members can legitimately perform a cost-benefit analysis when deciding the extent of enforcement and can also deduct from the amount of royalties eventually paid to IP owners the administrative costs relating to enforcement. Eventually, all disputes relating to the functioning and application of the TRIPs Agreement among WTO Members can be submitted to the WTO dispute settlement process.

5 Dispute settlement, transparency, and plurilateral agreements

The WTO dispute settlement system[1] constitutes a *prima facie* departure from the corresponding GATT system in that it provides for compulsory third party adjudication and also introduces, for the first time in the world trading system, a two instances-system of adjudication. The latter was a true innovation. Robert Hudec's monumental 1993 study amply shows that WTO Members learned to live *de facto* in a compulsory third party adjudication system: with the exception of one instance, all requests for the establishment of a panel met an affirmative reaction; the overwhelming majority of all reports were adopted; the majority of all reports adopted were implemented.[2] Of course, this study does not answer the question of how states would have behaved if there had been *de jure* compulsory third party adjudication as early as 1948. It could, for instance, be argued that some states, fearing a rejection, did not bother to request establishment of a panel. Still, these types of arguments do not cast doubt on the validity of Hudec's overall conclusions: the very low costs, in the majority of cases, associated with a request to establish a panel cannot reasonably act as a deterrent.

In today's world, trade, and to a lesser extent, the law of the sea, are the only two operational examples in international relations of compulsory third party adjudication. Following Hudec's argument, this illustrates the positive effect that GATT pragmatism has had on the shaping of dispute settlement. Many critics of the GATT 1947 were quick to point to the fact that consensus (needed to establish a panel; to adopt a report; and to allow countermeasures in case of non-implementation of adopted reports) was a big obstacle to a rules-oriented system. The benefit of consensus in generating legitimacy was too often ignored. The dispute settlement process from 1948–95 was legitimized by acceptance of decisions by contracting parties that were on the losing end in panel cases.[3]

Compulsory third party adjudication

The WTO Members adopted during the Uruguay Round the *Dispute Settlement Understanding* (DSU) which, together with a number of other specific provisions (*lex specialis*) mentioned in its Annexes, aims to govern adjudication at the WTO.[4] Art. 23.2 DSU is the dominant obligation in that it provides that WTO Members can resolve their disputes only through the use of the DSU procedures. The word "exclusively," reflected in the body of the DSU, has a double legal impact:

1 on the one hand, it ensures respect that no one should unilaterally define illegalities as to the trade practices of its partners;
2 on the other, it ensures that trading partners cannot submit their disputes to a forum other than the WTO forum.[5]

Two phases and two instances

As stated above, the DSU, with the advent of the AB, introduces a two-instances system. The AB, being a permanent body composed of renowned experts, was seen as a definitive departure from a diplomacy-oriented jurisprudence.[6] To move, however, to WTO "courts" (the second phase), WTO Members must first exhaust bilateral consultations (the first phase of WTO adjudication). In what follows, we explain the mechanics of WTO adjudication through a "fiction" dispute.

Assume that Consumeria (*C*) believes that Produceria (*P*) is violating its WTO obligations. Assume further that Freeridia (*F*), Systemia (*S*) and Defensia (*D*) have an interest in the dispute between the two countries. The first step, how *C* came to find out about *P*-policies, is not an issue of concern for WTO law. It is a domestic concern. Typically (in most western democracies), external relations are not an issue where branches of the government other than the executive have a lot to say. Some WTO Members have enacted domestic statutes (the *Trade Barriers Regulation* in the European Community and the *Section 301* in the United States), whereby the executive binds its discretion (to a varying degree) and accepts under conditions to represent private interests before the WTO. Since the WTO is a government-to-government contract where only governments can act as complainants and/or defendants, such instruments are necessary for private parties, affected by foreign governments' behavior, to ensure that their concerns will be heard. Art. 1 DSU makes it clear that the only form of dispute that can exist for the purposes of the DSU is that between two

WTO Members. Hence, *a contrario*, no WTO Member can act against a decision by the WTO membership taken by a Committee, a Council, etc.

Next, *C* will request from *P* to consult bilaterally on a defined issue and will notify its request for consultations to the WTO (Art. 4 DSU). At that stage *F*, *S* and *D* will have to weigh their options, assuming they want to participate. *F*, *S* and *D* can participate either by submitting a new request for consultations becoming co-complainants or as third parties – assuming the request for consultations is based on Article XXII.1 of the GATT, Article XXII.1 of the GATS or the corresponding provisions (Art. 4.11 DSU). There is no possibility for anyone to participate as co-defendant. Assuming they want to participate as third parties, they can do so only if *P* concedes to their request. If *P* does not, then they will have to start their own proceedings by submitting a new request for consultations. Let us assume that both *F* and *S* want to participate as third parties but *P* accepts only *F* under this capacity. Let us further assume that *S* sides with the arguments by *C*, whereas *D* sides with the arguments by *P*. *F* will participate as third party, *S* will start anew its own proceedings (on the same subject matter) against *P*, and *D* will await the results of consultations without participating. If during consultations, *C*, *F* and *P* fail to reach an amiable solution, 60 days after their initiation (or any other day thereafter), *C* (or *S*, or both as the case may be) can request the establishment of a panel. It could be that one of the two complainants reaches a solution and the other does not. If this is the case, the bilaterally reached solution will have to be notified to the WTO and provided that it is WTO-consistent (assuming no one raises a concern to this effect), their dispute will be over (Art. 3.6 DSU). For the purposes of our example, let us assume that neither *S* nor *C* reached such a solution with *P*.

The subsequent step is that *C* and *S* will submit a request to the WTO for the establishment of the panel. From a legal perspective the request for establishment is very important since, according to standing case law, WTO Members cannot add to the claims reflected in this document. On the other hand, if some claims are indiscernible, they will be thwarted by the Panel (Art. 6.2 DSU). At this stage, *F* (assuming that it has presented a new request for consultations and 60 days have passed without a solution) might request a new panel and that the two panel proceedings be merged. Art. 9 DSU allows for such procedures, but in practice, it all depends on the willingness of the parties concerned. Let us assume that now *P* agrees to *F*'s request, so we have now one merged panel where *S*, *F* and *C* act as complainants and *P* as defendant.

The panel is an *ad hoc* organ composed of three members. Its members are chosen either from a roster kept with the WTO Secretariat or can even be chosen outside the roster. If the parties cannot agree to the composition of the panel, then the Director-General of the WTO will fill the gaps (by adding, one, two or even all three members of the panel depending on the extent of the disagreement between the parties to the dispute). The panel, assisted by the WTO Secretariat, after consulting with the parties, will adopt its own working procedures and following two meetings with the parties will issue, first, an interim report, and within six months and at any rate within no more than nine months (Art. 12.8 and 12.9 DSU) will issue its final report. The panel has discovery powers (Art. 13 DSU) but cannot use them to extend its conclusions beyond what has been requested by the complainant(s). Third parties can participate in the panel proceedings provided that they can show substantial interest (in our example, this is what *D* will do, following Art. 10 DSU). Case law has now made it clear that non-WTO Members (usually, non-governmental organizations, NGOs) can participate with amicus curiae briefs. Third parties have the right to participate in the first meeting of the panel. The panel's work can be suspended for not more than a year (Art. 12.12 DSU). During the panel procedure, parties can reach an amicable solution and interrupt the panel process. If Art. 3.6 DSU, as indicated above, has been respected, the amicable solution reached will amount to the end of the procedure.

Let us assume for the purposes of our example, that the panel at hand accepts the complaint. *P* can appeal the report before the AB. The AB is a standing organ composed of seven members and assisted by its own Secretariat. It discusses cases and adjudicates disputes in divisions of three members. AB members are elected for four years, renewable once. Their mandate is to examine only the legal issues discussed in a panel report and decide the case at last resort. They have to render their decision within 60 and in no case longer than 90 days (Art. 17.5 DSU).

Assuming that the panel and the AB find violations, *P* will be requested to bring immediately its measures into compliance with its international obligations. The DSU allows for the possibility to provide *P* with a reasonable period of time (RPT) during which to do so. In practice, use of RPT is quite frequent. The extent of the RPT will be decided either through agreement between the parties or through recourse to an Arbitrator (Art. 21.3 DSU).

P does not necessarily have specific guidance as to what to do during the RPT. The usual WTO remedy is a recommendation for *P* to bring its measures into compliance without any further specifications as to what to do. Panels and/or the AB might add suggestions, that is provide *P* with specific guidance as to what to do (Art. 19 DSU). Case law has clarified that suggestions are not binding and very often panels, even if requested to do so, have refused to suggest ways for WTO Members that are in violation of their obligations to bring their measures into compliance. Recommendations remain the predominant ruling of panels and the AB, if they find violations of the WTO. Greater use of suggestions would have the benefit that they establish an irrefutable presumption of compliance if they are followed.

As a result of the limited guidance, it could very often be the case that parties disagree whether implementing activity has been sufficient for the addressee of the recommendation to bring its measures into compliance. If *P* in our example does nothing during the RPT, then obviously the illegality persists and the complainants can act against it. If P, however, does something, it could very well be the case that its actions are deemed unsatisfactory by *F*, *S* and *C* (or at least by some of them). Of course, if all three or some of them agree with *P*'s implementing activities, then, provided that Art. 3.6 DSU has been complied with, the case is over. Now assume for our discussion that *P* does something and all three complainants believe that this something is not enough.

In application of the maxim embedded in Art. 23.2 DSU, *F*, *S* and *C* will have to (assuming they want to continue their legal battle) submit the case to a compliance panel (Art. 21.5 DSU). Composition-wise, a compliance panel, whenever feasible, will be composed of the members of the original panel. Its mandate is to respond to one question: is what *P* did during the RPT sufficient for *P* to have brought its measures into compliance with its obligations? Within 90 days it must render its report which can be appealed. WTO practice shows that more than one compliance panel can be instituted on the same dispute.[7] Compensation may be provided to the winning party, but is mostly never provided.

Assuming that the compliance panel and AB report (if need be) still find that *P* is wrong since it did not do enough to remove the original illegality, *S*, *F* and *C* will have the right to request countermeasures. They can request countermeasures[8] in any field of their interest: if, for example, faced with a violation in the field of goods, they can request retaliation in the field of services or TRIPs.[9] What the complainants will have to obey is strict equivalence between the damage done and the extent of countermeasures requested (Art. 22.4 DSU).[10] Although Art. 22.1 DSU makes it clear that WTO countermeasures can take the form of either suspension of concessions or any other obligations, so far, only the former have been authorized.[11] If the parties to the dispute agree on the level of countermeasures, the Arbitrators (if feasible, the members of the original panel) will decide on first and last resort. Countermeasures have been imposed on three occasions so far. They are generally viewed as counter-productive by developing countries which, during the Doha Round, tabled specific proposals to address this issue.[12]

The WTO courts have become the busiest international bodies adjudicating government-to-government disputes. As of early 2006, over 350 consultations had been requested, of which more than 100 led to the completion of a panel report (and over 70 AB reports had been issued). Although some disputes find settlement outside the confines of the WTO, it is a widely used instrument (by any standard).

A comprehensive data set that covers disputes from the genesis of the WTO until the end of 2005 suggests that the share of import trade is the most relevant proxy explaining the number of appearances of a WTO Member as defendant, the United States and the EC topping the list in this respect.[13] By contrast, the share of export trade is not as reliable a proxy, the United States and the EC lagging slightly behind the numbers that a one-to-one relationship would have yielded. Administrative capacity seems to play an important role: the EC and the United States are omnipresent in disputes either as complainants, or defendants or third parties. LDCs are almost totally absent.

Transparency, Art. X GATT

There are various provisions in the covered agreements which deal with transparency. From its birth, the WTO has, in marked difference to the GATT, taken some steps towards enhancing transparency of the institution, but also of its Members. We have already dealt with issues concerning transparency of the institution in various chapters of this volume. In this chapter, we deal only with the general transparency obligations embedded in Art. X GATT and the Trade Policy Review Mechanism (TPRM).

Art. X GATT[14] imposes a general transparency obligation on WTO Members. It imposes the following obligations:

1   An obligation to publish all laws, as well as administrative and judicial decisions of general application affecting trade. Since it is quite difficult to exclude *a priori* that a state act will have an effect on trade, the coverage of Art. X GATT hinges on the interpretation of the term *general application* (Art. X.1 GATT).

2 A *standstill* obligation: state acts covered by the first paragraph will not be enforced before their publication, if they represent a new or more burdensome requirement on imports (Art. X.2 GATT).

3 An obligation that state acts covered in the first paragraph are administered in a uniform, reasonable, and impartial manner (Art. X.3 GATT).

The AB, in its report on *US – Underwear*, understood the transparency obligation embedded in Art. X GATT as a due process obligation: traders affected by laws coming under the purview of Art. X GATT should be aware of their substantive content. This is, in the AB's view, the quintessential legal nature of Art. X GATT (p. 21):

> Article X.2, General Agreement, may be seen to embody a principle of fundamental importance – that of promoting full disclosure of governmental acts affecting Members and private persons and enterprises, whether of domestic or foreign nationality. The relevant policy principle is widely known as the principle of transparency and has obviously due process dimensions. The essential implication is that Members and other persons affected, or likely to be affected, by governmental measures imposing restraints, requirements and other burdens, should have a reasonable opportunity to acquire authentic information about such measures and accordingly to protect and adjust their activities or alternatively to seek modification of such measures.

One should not, however, interpret this passage as the institutional acknowledgment of the principle of direct effect of Art. X GATT.[15] It is simply the explanation of its practical implications: it is traders who need to be fully aware of the transaction costs when doing business with foreign nations. The panel report on *Argentina – Hides and Leather* noted in this respect (§ 11.76):

> Indeed, the focus is on the treatment accorded by government authorities to the traders in question. This is explicit in Article X.1 which requires, *inter alia*, that all provisions "shall be published promptly in such a manner as to enable governments and *traders* to become acquainted with them" (emphasis added). While it is normal that the GATT 1994 should require this sort of transparency between Members, it is significant that Article X.1 goes further and specifically references the importance of transparency to individual traders.

This panel report further discussed the legal relationship between the various paragraphs of Art. X GATT. It acknowledged to this effect, that the satisfaction of the first paragraph of Art. X GATT is a threshold issue for a review of a claim under Art. X.3 GATT. The same panel recognized that Art. X GATT does not reflect a discrimination test: WTO Members must respect this obligation irrespective of whether discriminatory effects result or not. The *Argentina – Hides and Leather* panel also dismissed an argument that Art. X GATT should apply only to unpublished acts (§ 11.71). In its view, such an interpretation would run counter to the explicit wording of Art. X.1 GATT. As a result, both WTO Members that have *not* published an act coming under the purview of Art. X GATT, as well as those that do publish but without respecting its requirements, violate Art. X GATT.

The panel report on *Dominican Republic – Importation and Sale of Cigarettes* made clear that not only positive actions, but *omissions* too can come under scrutiny in the context of the review regarding the consistency of a specific law, regulation, etc. with Art. X.3 GATT (§ 7.379). In the case at hand, Honduras challenged the practice by the Dominican Republic to avoid calculating the imposition of a tax on imported cigarettes based on one of the three methods reflected under the Dominican law (§ 7.387). Instead, the Dominican Republic, on its own admission, was calculating the amount of imposition based on variables other than those published in the relevant generally applicable law. That is, the Dominican Republic had not included in its publication of laws variables used for the calculation of the imposition in this respect. Such an omission constituted, in the panel's view, an unreasonable administration of its laws (§ 7.388).

Trade Policy Review Mechanism

During the Uruguay Round, a negotiating group named "Functioning of the GATT" (the FOGs group in GATT parlance) recommended the creation of a surveillance mechanism whereby the WTO Secretariat would periodically review national trade policies. The FOGs decision (GATT Doc. L/6490 of 13 April 1989) does not go into great details as to the organization of the proposed surveillance exercise. This was done in a more "learning by doing" fashion, based on the experience acquired through practice. The 1989 decision, however, gave birth to the WTO Trade Policy Review Mechanism (TPRM). This subjects all WTO Members to periodic review, the frequency depending on the relative importance of a Member in world trade.

Large traders such as the EC and the US are reviewed on a bi-annual basis; some developing countries and transition economies have yet to be reviewed, 10 years after the entry into force of the WTO. It is the latter countries that presumably would benefit the most from a review, suggesting that the sequencing may be inappropriate. A good case can be made that much more attention should focus on the poorer and smaller WTO Members and less on the largest traders, as the former will be subject to much less regular scrutiny by trading partners. Traders have an incentive to monitor policies of large countries and to initiate dispute settlement proceedings in cases where they perceive a violation of the WTO to have occurred. Such incentives are much weaker if a country is very small or very poor.

Although there are inherent limits to the TPRM exercise as the WTO Secretariat does not have the legal power to interpret the WTO Agreement – so that reports cannot reflect legal assessments as to the consistency of national policies with the overarching WTO obligations – the TPRM is an important exercise in transparency. WTO Secretariat reports are supposed to lay out all pertinent information regarding prevailing national trade policies and their implementation. In this sense, reports are a natural complement to many other transparency provisions in the WTO (chief among them being Art. X GATT and Art. III GATS on publication of all trade laws of general application).

As of January 2006, the TPRM had conducted 212 reviews since its formation (WTO Doc. WT/TPR/173, 8 November 2005), covering 123 Members (out of 148 at that time), counting the European Union as one. Given a decision to focus more attention on reviews of LDCs, a total of 23 such reviews were completed between 1998 and 2005. In order to expand the number of reports, a number of reviews of developing countries are being prepared with the assistance of consultants. Trade Policy Reviews of LDCs have increasingly performed a technical assistance function, aiming in part to increase the understanding of prevailing trade policies and their relationship with the WTO Agreements. Since 2000, the review process for an LDC includes a three-to-four-day seminar for local officials on the WTO and the trade policy review exercise.

Plurilateral agreements

While the multilateral agreements contained in the WTO are binding on all Members, the WTO also provides for the negotiation of agreements to which participation is optional. At the time of the entry into force of the WTO there were four such "plurilateral" agreements:

1   the International Dairy Agreement;
2   the International Bovine Meat Agreement;
3   the Agreement on Trade in Civil Aircraft; and
4   the Government Procurement Agreement (GPA).

The provisions of plurilateral agreements bind only those WTO Members that accept them:

> The agreements and associated legal instruments included in Annex 4 (hereinafter referred to as "Plurilateral Trade Agreements") are also part of this Agreement for those Members that have accepted them, and are binding on those Members. The Plurilateral Trade Agreements do not create either obligations or rights for Members that have not accepted them.
>
> (Art. II.3 WTO)

The Dairy and Bovine Meat agreements were legacies of the Tokyo Round. They comprised non-binding commitments to share information on the state of the world market for these products.[16] They expired on 31 December 1997. At the time of writing, there are therefore only two plurilateral agreements in force. Of these, the Agreement on Trade in Civil Aircraft, also a product of the Tokyo Round, is mostly redundant in that its disciplines were incorporated in the Uruguay Round SCM Agreement.[17]

The Government Procurement Agreement (GPA)

The GPA was first negotiated during the Tokyo Round, motivated by the fact that Art. III.8 GATT excludes procurement from the national treatment obligation. It was subsequently extended to cover services as well (recall that Art. XIII GATS excludes procurement of services from national treatment). The GPA covers purchases of governments where there is no intention to re-sell. As such, its obligations are to be distinguished, for example, from the obligations imposed on governments when they have recourse to state trading (Art. XVII GATT). Governmental and non-governmental entities (e.g., state-owned firms) scheduled by GPA signatories are required to purchase on a non-discriminatory basis.

Membership is limited: signatories span Canada, the European Community (25 members), Hong Kong, China, Iceland, Israel, Japan, Korea, Liechtenstein, the Netherlands with respect to Aruba, Norway, Singapore, Switzerland, and the United States. No developing countries joined its ranks during the period 1995–2005. This reflects a mix of factors, including a perceived lack of direct benefits because developing countries are pursuing procurement reform unilaterally; an absence of export interests; the administrative costs associated with compliance – notification, reporting, procedures, etc.; and a desire to use procurement policies as an instrument of industrial and redistributive policy, i.e., as a mechanism through which governments can promote the interests of domestic firms, disadvantaged ethnic or religious groups, minorities, or regions within the country.

To encourage participation by developing countries, Art. V.1 GPA contains a best endeavor clause, calling on signatories to duly take into account the need of developing countries to safeguard their balance of payments position; to promote the establishment of domestic industries; to support their industrial units; and to encourage their development through arrangements among developing countries. Moreover, Art. V.3 GPA states that:

> With a view to ensuring that developing countries are able to adhere to this Agreement on terms consistent with their development, financial and trade needs, the objectives listed in paragraph 1 shall be duly taken into account in the course of negotiations with respect to the procurement of developing countries to be covered by the provisions of this Agreement. Developed countries, in the preparation of their coverage lists under the provisions of this Agreement, shall endeavor to include entities procuring products and services of export interest to developing countries.

Notwithstanding their intention of providing flexibility to developing countries, these provisions have had little success in expanding membership. The countries that were in the process of negotiating accession – Albania, Bulgaria, Chinese Taipei, Georgia, Jordan, Kyrgyz Republic, Moldova, Oman and Panama – all acceded to the WTO after 1995 and were asked to agree to launch such negotiations as part of their accession process.

The GPA legal disciplines

GPA disciplines apply to any law, regulation, procedure or practice regarding any procurement by entities listed in Appendix 1 to the Agreement (Art. I). Appendix 1 is divided into five Annexes, covering central government entities (Annex 1); sub-central government entities (Annex 2); all other entities that procure in accordance with the provisions of this Agreement (Annex 3); entities procuring services (Annex 4); and entities procuring construction services (Annex 5). Hence, the GPA covers both goods and services.[18] Each signatory schedules entities under each of the five Annexes for which GPA obligations apply. The Annexes also specify the applicable threshold-value under which the GPA rules do not need to be applied.

Non-discrimination is the core obligation of the GPA (Art. III). It covers both MFN and national treatment:

> With respect to all laws, regulations, procedures and practices regarding government procurement covered by this Agreement, each Party shall provide immediately and unconditionally to the products, services and suppliers of other Parties offering products and services of the Parties, treatment no less favorable than: (a) that accorded to domestic producers, services and suppliers; and (b) that accorded to products, services and suppliers of any other Party.
>
> (Art. III GPA)

Whereas Art. III.1 GPA binds parties to the GPA, Art. III.2 GPA imposes on parties the additional obligation to ensure that their entities will observe the non-discrimination principle. The non-discrimination obligation binds the GPA signatories with respect to any tendering procedure that they might choose to follow for contracts and entities coming under the purview of the GPA. Rules to determine the origin of suppliers are not defined by the GPA; each Member may determine this unilaterally – all that it is obliged to do is to apply it consistently with the national treatment obligation. As is the case in both GATT and GATS, the GPA contains exceptions to pursue national security, public morals, order and safety objectives (Art. XXIII GPA).

Tendering procedures

The GPA distinguishes between four different tendering procedures:

1 *open tendering procedures*, whereby, by virtue of Art. VII.3(a) GPA, any interested party may apply;
2 *selective tendering procedures*, whereby only few suppliers are invited by the entity to participate (provided that the relevant provisions of the GPA, Art. X, and Art. VII.3(b), have been respected). To ensure that these procedures will not serve as a gateway to protectionist behavior, the procuring entities are required to invite

the maximum number of entities to submit a tender. Art. VIII GPA includes safeguards to ensure that conditions for qualification do not discriminate against foreign suppliers. Moreover, by virtue of Art. IX.9 GPA, procuring entities are required to publish on a yearly basis the list of suppliers that qualify for these procedures, as well as the criteria that new suppliers are required to meet for their inclusion on the list;

3 *limited tendering procedures*, whereby an entity may, by virtue of Art. VII.3(c) GPA, contact suppliers individually provided that the relevant provisions of the GPA (Art. XV) are respected. Art. XV GPA reserves the possibility to have recourse to *limited* tendering in carefully drafted cases, such as cases of urgency, or cases where no response to an open and/or selective procedure has been registered, or cases where the product or service purchased can only be purchased from one supplier.

4 *Negotiations* between the procuring entity and economic operators – this is subject to strict conditions laid down in Art. XIV GPA (for example, when it is clear that no one tender is the most advantageous and subject to the non-discrimination discipline).

The rank ordering of these procedures and the types of criteria that are embodied in the GPA are very similar to – and consistent with – the UNCITRAL model law on procurement and the guidelines that are applied by the World Bank and other development banks in their procurement.[19]

6 Developing countries and the WTO

Developing countries have played a prominent role in the evolution of the trading system. Concerns regarding the appropriateness of GATT disciplines and processes led to perceptions that they could not compete for export markets on an equal basis with developed countries. As noted previously, this led to a variety of provisions calling for preferential access to major markets and less than full reciprocity in negotiations. As noted in the panel report on *EC – Tariff Preferences*:

> During the Second Session of UNCTAD, on 26 March 1968, a Resolution was adopted on "Expansion and Diversification of Exports and Manufactures and Semi-manufactures of Developing Countries" (Resolution 21 (II)). In this Resolution, UNCTAD agreed to the "early establishment of a mutually acceptable system of generalized, non-reciprocal and non-discriminatory preferences which would be beneficial to the developing countries" and established a Special Committee on Preferences as a subsidiary organ of the Trade and Development Board, with a mandate to settle the details of the GSP arrangements. In 1970, UNCTAD's Special Committee on Preferences adopted Agreed Conclusions which set up the agreed details of the GSP arrangement. UNCTAD's Trade and Development Board took note of these Agreed Conclusions on 13 January 1970. In accordance with the Agreed Conclusions, certain developed GATT contracting parties sought a waiver for the GSP from the GATT Council. The GATT granted a 10-year waiver on 25 June 1971. Before the expiry of this waiver, the CONTRACTING PARTIES adopted a decision on "Differential and More Favorable Treatment, Reciprocity and Fuller Participation of Developing Countries" (the "Enabling Clause") on 28 November 1979.

The Enabling Clause provides the legal cover for deviations from MFN tariffs in favor of developing countries to become a permanent feature of the GATT/WTO.

Some historical background

Debates on how the trading system should relate to the concerns of developing nations have recurred since the establishment of the GATT in 1947. The first time a comprehensive discussion on trade and development took place in the GATT was in 1958 with the circulation of the *Haberler Report*. This report examined the claim that GATT rules on trade liberalization would not necessarily work to the advantage of developing countries. It concluded that there was some justification for this view,[1] noting that protectionist agricultural policies of developed nations were a contributory factor to lower and more volatile commodity prices. The United States had obtained a waiver in 1955 that allowed substantial subsidization of farm production, while the EC imposed policies that made its farm market practically impenetrable. Through a variable levy system, imported products were burdened with a customs duty that equaled the difference between the world and the European price. The debates of the late 1950s are quite similar to those of today.

The consistency of the EC regime with GATT rules was doubtful at best. Some of its aspects were challenged, but many were not. The EC could point to Art. XI.2 GATT which allows for limited exceptions from the general prohibition to ban QRs; it also benefited from the indulgence of major trading partners who did not want to question the EC integration process, which was seen as an important initiative to cement the peace in Europe. Moreover, the US was not in a good position to throw stones in light of the waiver they had previously obtained.

The *Haberler Report* made a series of recommendations, including reductions in farm protectionism in developed nations. Most importantly, it sensitized GATT contracting parties to the fact that not all stood to gain equally from the trade regime, and that actions were needed to address the concerns of those who were being left behind.

During the Kennedy Round (1962–67), one of the negotiating groups, the *Committee on Legal and Institutional Framework of GATT in Relation to Less-Developed Countries* worked on a text on Trade and Development. This text was finalized in a Special Session of the CON-TRACTING PARTIES, held from 17 November 1964 to 8 February 1965, and was added to the GATT by virtue of an amending protocol as Part IV of the GATT. Part IV came into effect on 27 June 1966.

Part IV comprises three "best endeavor" clauses. Art. XXXVI GATT, § 8, introduces the principle of non-reciprocity for developing countries:[2]

> The developed contracting parties do not expect reciprocity for commitments made by them in trade negotiations to reduce or remove tariffs and other barriers to the trade of less-developed contracting parties.

An Interpretative Note ad Art. XXXVI GATT goes on to specify that:

> It is understood that the phrase "do not expect reciprocity" means, in accordance with the objectives set forth in this Article, that the less-developed contracting parties should not be expected, in the course of trade negotiations, to make contributions which are inconsistent with their individual development, financial and trade needs, taking into consideration past trade developments.

During the final stages of the Kennedy Round, this provision was further interpreted as follows:

> There will, therefore, be no balancing of concessions granted on products of interest to developing countries by developed participants on the one hand and the contribution which developing participants would make to the objective of trade liberalization on the other and which it is agreed should be considered in the light of the development, financial and trade needs of developing countries themselves. It is, therefore, recognized that the developing countries themselves must decide what contributions they can make.[3]

The second new clause, Art. XXXVII GATT, recommended various actions that developed states should undertake in order to help developing countries. Chief among these was an incitation to reduce high tariffs (what came to be called tariff peaks) and tariff escalation: the gap between (high) barriers on processed goods, and (low) barriers on primary, unprocessed products. Ever since, developing countries have sought to reduce tariff peaks in major export markets. Art. XXXVII also called on developed countries, when imposing countervailing or antidumping duties, or safeguard measures, to "have special regard to the trade interests" of developing countries and "explore all

possibilities of constructive remedies before applying such measures."
In the WTO antidumping agreement this provision is now a binding
legal obligation.

The third element of Part IV, Art. XXXVIII GATT was meant to
provide the institutional vehicle to implement the other two provisions
of Part IV, including collaboration with the United Nations and its
organs and agencies and monitoring of the rate of growth of the trade
of developing countries.

In addition to the adoption of Part IV, a Committee on Trade and
Development was established in 1964. Its mandate was to review the
application of the provisions of Part IV. Also in 1964, the International Trade Centre (ITC) was established, with the aim of promoting
trade of developing countries. The ITC subsequently became a joint
agency of UNCTAD and GATT. It is today a source of information
and technical assistance for export development, focusing in particular
on the private sector in developing countries (in contrast to
UNCTAD and WTO, where the focus is solely on governments).

The 1979 Enabling Clause essentially reproduces the ideas and
concepts contained in Part IV of the GATT, providing the legal basis
for developed GATT/WTO Members to accord preferential access to
their markets for developing country exporters. The Enabling Clause
became an integral part of the GATT by virtue of Art. 1(b)(iv) of
GATT 1994. In the view of the AB (report on *EC – Preferences* § 99)
the Enabling Clause constitutes an exception to Art. I GATT,
implying that it takes precedence over Art. I if there is a conflict
between the two provisions (§ 102).

As noted in Chapter 3, the term *developing countries* is nowhere
defined in the GATT/WTO. In practice, WTO Members choose for
themselves whether they are developing. This has generally not led to
many challenges.[4] Practice suggests that almost all OECD members
are considered to be developed countries, and thus do not benefit
from inclusion in GSP schemes.[5]

Non-discrimination in the context of the Enabling Clause

The 2003 panel report on *European Communities – Conditions for the
Granting of Tariff Preferences to Developing Countries* (WTO Doc. WT/
DS246/R) accepted that the Enabling Clause, because it provides preferential treatment to products of developing countries only, is an exception to Art. I.1 GATT (§ 7.39). In the case at hand, India and Pakistan
both benefited from the EC GSP. Pakistan, however, received extra
preferences because it qualified under the so-called *Drug Arrangements*,

a scheme aimed at compensating those WTO Members adopting active policies against drug production and trafficking. India complained that by discriminating in favor of Pakistani imports, the EC was in violation of Art. I.1 GATT, a point accepted by the panel (§ 7.60). The panel then went on to examine to what extent recourse to the Enabling Clause could be offered as justification. In the panel's view, the Enabling Clause requires that Members, absent *a priori* limitations (cases where some developing countries are excluded altogether from GSP programs), must give identical tariff preferences under GSP schemes to all developing countries without any differentiation (by virtue of the term "non-discriminatory" in footnote 3 of the Enabling Clause).

The AB reversed the panel's findings in this respect. It started its analysis (§ 157) by pointing to the terms used in § 3(c) of the Enabling Clause, which specifies that "differential and more favorable treatment" provided under the Enabling Clause:

> shall in the case of such treatment accorded by developed contracting parties to developing countries be designed and, if necessary, modified, to respond positively to the development, financial and trade needs of developing countries.

In its view, this paragraph made it plain that development needs are not necessarily shared to the same extent by all developing countries (§ 162),[6] and, responding to such needs, would consequently require that a GSP scheme may be "non-discriminatory" even if "identical" tariff treatment is not accorded to all GSP beneficiaries (§ 165). As a result, additional preferences cannot be outright excluded (§ 169). It went on to rule that:

> in granting such differential tariff treatment, however, preference-granting countries are required, by virtue of the term "non-discriminatory," to ensure that identical treatment is available to all similarly-situated GSP beneficiaries, that is, to all GSP beneficiaries that have the "development, financial and trade needs" to which the treatment in question is intended to respond.
>
> (§ 173)

Applying its test to the specific case, the AB found that the Drug Arrangements were not WTO-consistent, since the European Community laid down a closed list of beneficiaries (§§ 180, 187). For its scheme to be deemed WTO-consistent, the European Community, in the AB's view, would have to modify its current Regulation so as to ensure that it reflects "criteria or standards to provide a basis for distinguishing beneficiaries under the Drug Arrangements from other GSP beneficiaries" (§ 188).

Accordingly, WTO Members can distinguish between recipients of preferences between developing countries, provided that they have established criteria to that effect. The AB thus opened the door to extra preferences, but did not provide any principles which could serve as benchmark to distinguish between acceptable and (eventually) unacceptable criteria, following which, extra preferences can be legitimately granted. Moreover, it is unclear whether such criteria should be unilaterally defined, or whether they should be the outcome of some consensus between donor and recipient countries.

Differential and more favorable treatment in practice

In practice, trade preferences have been the dominant dimension of special and differential treatment (SDT) provided under the cover of the Enabling Clause. Preferences were granted as a form of development assistance – the aim being to help expand and diversify exports. Space constraints prohibit a lengthy discussion, but the empirical literature suggests that preferences have not been able to assist the poorest countries today very much.[7] The original intention of preferences was not to transfer resources directly but rather to help in the development of exports. Preferential access may create additional incentives to export, but does so at the expense of other, less- or non-preferred countries, involves administrative costs – such as rules of origin – that reduce the benefits, and may result in part of the associated rents being captured by importers if the latter have some market power. It also does nothing to help countries deal with supply-side constraints. The transfers implied by current preferential access programs are limited, and very specific to a small number of countries that have benefited from quota-determined access to highly distorted markets such as bananas and sugar. It should also be recognized that deep preferences will imply MFN liberalization – a key objective of the WTO – and will result in preference erosion. Recipient developing countries then have an incentive to oppose MFN liberalization. The *EC – Tariff Preferences* dispute illustrated that rich countries (in this case, the EU) essentially pay preferred countries such as Pakistan and other beneficiaries of its Drug Arrangement preferences with money obtained from other developing countries, as the trade diversions generated by the preferences are in products all developing countries produce.[8]

Many of the poorest countries of today have not managed to diversify and expand exports even *with* the preferences they receive, because they lack the necessary supply capacity or are not competitive. This suggests that granting more preferences to the poorest countries – for example, extending preference programs for poor countries to large emerging markets – is unlikely to yield much benefit. However, this was the path taken at the Hong Kong WTO Ministerial. Developed country Members agreed to provide duty-free and quota-free market access for products originating from LDCs by 2008 or no later than the start of the implementation period of the Doha Round. Developing countries in a position to do so are to do likewise. Even though the initiative is limited to LDCs – mostly countries with limited supply capacity – because of resistance in some OECD countries to granting access to clothing, leather and rice, the free market access commitments may be limited to 97 percent of tariff lines. This limitation potentially significantly undermines the value of the commitment for LDCs. For example, over 70 percent of Bangladesh's exports to the US are covered by only 70 tariff lines, which together account for less than 1 percent of all US tariff lines.[9] Only 39 tariff lines account for 76 percent of Cambodia's exports to the US.

Turning to SDT for WTO rules, the traditional approach to determining the reach of WTO disciplines for developing countries is through exceptions, often temporary, and longer transition periods. In assessing the value of these exceptions, it is important to distinguish between trade policy and other domestic policies as development tools. There are numerous potential rationales for government intervention, including the provision of public goods and services, to redistribute income, and to address market failures. Trade policy is a tool of raising revenue and to redistribute income. However, one does not need SDT to justify the use of tariffs for revenue purposes, and trade policy is generally an inefficient and nontransparent tool to redistribute incomes. Moreover, the case for trade policy to address market failures is particularly weak. Economic theory argues that policy interventions should directly target the source of the failure. Trade policy will rarely do so. If trade policies are used, there is a clear efficiency ranking of instruments, with quotas and quota-like instruments being particularly costly. WTO rules that impose disciplines on the use of less efficient instruments will benefit consumers and exporters in developing countries and enhance global welfare. The implication is that a good case can be made that the basic trade policy rules of the WTO make sense for all countries, both developed and developing.

This is not to deny the existence of market failures or the need for governments to provide public goods and engage in income redistribution. Nor does it imply that governments should not seek to use domestic regulation and tax/subsidies to encourage local learning, protect the environment, etc. But trade policy is simply not the best instrument to pursue such objectives. Indeed, often it will be completely ineffective. What is needed is greater effort to assist developing country governments to attain their development objectives through more effective and efficient instruments. Development assistance to bolster trade capacity can be one way to encourage the use of alternative instruments, a subject we return to in Chapter 7.

7 Whither the trading system after Doha?

Deadlock as an opportunity?

The WTO is one of the most successful multilateral institutions of the post-1945 period. Despite the absence of a central authority, cooperation has been sustained for over 50 years. Over time, the coverage of the institution has expanded, both in terms of scope and membership. The Uruguay Round was a watershed, expanding the trading system to cover two sectors, agriculture and textiles, that had effectively been removed from the GATT, and adding disciplines in two new areas, trade in services and intellectual property protection. In the latter half of the 1990s, there was substantial optimism that the WTO would further extend its coverage of domestic policies affecting trade and investment. However, initial efforts to do so in Seattle (1999) failed spectacularly. Despite the eventual successful launch of a new round in Doha in 2001, progress proved difficult.

There are many challenges confronting WTO Members. In our view, three stand out: (1) extending multilateral cooperation to domestic "behind the border" policies; (2) addressing concerns of developing countries that the trading system is "unbalanced"; and (3) dealing with the proliferation of preferential trade agreements. None of these challenges are new. Although subjects such as investment and competition policies could not be put on the Doha negotiating agenda, by definition, many services "trade policies" are regulatory and behind the border in nature. Moreover, many PTAs include disciplines on domestic regulatory policies, also suggesting that these are subjects that will not go away. The basic question here is whether and when harmonization is desirable.

TRIPs is the first example of an agreement that involves a significant element of policy harmonization. The inclusion of TRIPs in the WTO legal system has often been criticized. Although most economists accept there is an economic logic to IP protection,[1] the criticism is about the appropriateness of common minimum standards of IP protection for all countries. Experience to date does not suggest clear conclusions regarding the impact of TRIPs disciplines on individual Members, but both theory and economic history suggest harmonization is unlikely to be an optimal outcome for all countries, in particular, poor economies. Whatever the case may be, TRIPS greatly increased the awareness of many developing countries of the need to carefully scrutinize the likely impacts of agreements that entail regulatory harmonization.

Attaining trade liberalization through reciprocal bargaining requires a "negotiating set" that has something for everyone. While some traditional market access issues remain important – as discussed below – overall tariff barriers are now quite low in many countries. The average applied tariff in OECD countries is less than 5 percent, and the average tariff in developing countries is around 10 percent. This explains why countries have been seeking to expand the negotiating set by adding "behind the border" issues to link to sensitive areas such as agricultural reforms. Such linkage strategies may be effective, but can also be highly divisive, especially if a large subset of the membership is concerned that multilateral rules in the proposed area(s) might not be in their interest, or would do little to promote progress on the market access issues that matter most for them.

The reciprocity dynamics of the WTO negotiating process require that developing countries offer "enough" to OECD countries to induce them to take on the domestic interest groups that benefit from trade protection and vice versa. If there is little desire to engage on new issues, by necessity, the focus must be on trade policies for goods and services. The latter is inconsistent with the traditional developing country strategy of limited reciprocity and their desire for preferential access to OECD markets. There is still much scope for trade market access commitments – in both goods and services. In contrast to regulatory issues or demands for the stronger enforcement of rights to intangible assets (intellectual property, geographical indications) that may entail a zero-sum bargain (creation or protection of rents), the market access agenda implies trading "bads," so that there is a greater likelihood that all gain at the end of the day.

The case for exempting developing countries from liberalization is weak – own trade protection also hurts poor people in poor countries. But low-income countries with weak institutional capacity may not be able or may not benefit from implementing specific WTO agreements, especially if these require significant investment of scarce resources. A key need for the WTO to remain (become more) relevant to developing countries is that both market access for their products is improved further and that obligations are "tailored" appropriately to support the development process. At the same time the institution needs to be able to move forward and address issues that are of concern to more developed countries, including matters of a regulatory nature. A new framework for SDT in the WTO could help achieve both objectives.

As we write this, the Doha Round has stalled due to an inability to agree on negotiating modalities, in turn, reflecting fundamental differences on the scope of the WTO, the political strength of the farm lobby in the EU, Japan and the US, and difficulties in accommodating the demands of many developing countries on a variety of matters, ranging from preference erosion fears and demands for compensation to an unwillingness to offer reciprocity. In our view, a fundamental constraint that is stymieing cooperation is that the WTO Members have many objectives but are centering attention on only a small set of trade-related policies. There is only so much that trade and trade policy can achieve. A basic economic principle is that in most cases, for every objective, one needs a separate instrument. This insight suggests adding additional instruments to the mix may help promote further progress on trade liberalization and cooperation on rules.

Nascent steps have recently been taken to do exactly this, most notably via development assistance ("aid for trade") and additional monitoring of policy and "policy coherence." While many WTO Members have not shown a great willingness to consider measures to strengthen the WTO, there are positive signs. Whatever the ultimate fate of the Doha Round, it is clear that, absent changes to the "structure" of the WTO, the institution will find it difficult to achieve its objectives. In what follows, we distinguish between substantive trade policy and institutional questions, and suggest some elements of a possible way forward.

Key market access challenges

Market access is the bread and butter of the WTO, and is an area where the institution has been successful over time. It is often remarked that as a result of this success we are left with the "hard nuts" – sectors where interest groups are powerful and very effective in resisting liberalization.

Agriculture

Making further progress on reducing trade distorting policies in agriculture is critical both for the development prospects of many countries and for the credibility/relevance of the trading system. The majority of the population in developing countries tends to be rural and thus dependent, directly or indirectly, on this sector. And most WTO Members are developing. The fact that barriers to trade in agriculture are much higher than protection in general is a major source of discrimination against developing country farmers and those dependent on rural economies.[2]

Despite the fact that the inclusion of agricultural policy disciplines in the Uruguay Round was justifiably hailed as a major achievement, the commitments that were made – the ban and tariffication of QRs, minimum market access commitments for most protected products, reducing export subsidies and the aggregate measure of support – did not do much to lower agricultural protection. The effective level of protection has diminished little since the creation of the WTO, although the extent to which trade-distorting instruments were used – output-based subsidies and market price support did decline (from 83 to 66 percent of the total). Total net transfers from consumers and taxpayers to farmers in OECD countries equaled 37 percent of total farm revenue in 1986–88; in 2003, after implementation of all Uruguay commitments, they still amounted to 32 percent. The producer nominal protection coefficient (the ratio of prices received by producers to the border price) fell from 58 to 31 percent between 1986–88 and 2003 in the OECD, the number of active farmers declined over this period as well. As a result, support per farmer has continued to rise in many OECD countries – by 31 percent in the US and 60 percent in the EC.[3]

Highly distorting agricultural support policies in many OECD countries have a major detrimental effect on developing countries, including LDCs. Numerous analyses have documented the detrimental effects of OECD policies on developing countries. For example, *sugar* is one of the most policy-distorted of all commodities, with OECD protection rates frequently above 200 percent. Producers in those countries receive more than double the world market price. OECD support to sugar producers, of $6.4 billion per year, roughly equals developing country exports. US subsidies to *cotton* growers totaled $3.9 billion in 2003, three times US foreign aid to Africa. These subsidies depress world cotton prices by around 10–20 percent, cutting the income of poor farmers in West Africa, Central and South Asia, and poor countries around the world. In West Africa alone, where cotton is a critical cash crop for many small-scale and near-subsistence farmers, annual income losses for cotton growers are about $250 million a year.[4]

A major feature of the discrimination that is created by these poli-cies is that different developing countries are affected quite differen-tially. Some producers benefit from preferential access for some products, at the expense of other developing countries (e.g., Mauritius vs. Brazil on sugar); and some consumers in importing developing countries benefit from artificially low prices of some commodities. But, overall, the distortions created by OECD agricultural policies have negative repercussions on developing countries and are a major source of discriminatory bias in the world trading system today.

Tariff peaks and contingent protection

It is well known that the structure of protection today is biased against goods produced by developing countries – tariff peaks (rates of 15 percent or higher) tend to apply to labor-intensive products and sensitive agricultural goods in both high- and low-income countries. It is for this reason that a non-linear formula approach towards nego-tiating tariff cuts is particularly important for many developing coun-tries. The mechanics of such negotiations are well known to WTO Members – what is needed is political will on their part to apply a formula that cuts tariff peaks significantly. That in turn will require reciprocity on the part of larger developing countries. This is an area where the reciprocity dynamics should still be powerful enough to allow further liberalization to be achieved. However, as discussed below, doing more to address the inevitable adjustment costs for affected firms and households could have large payoffs in allowing deeper liberalization to occur.

The complex system of quotas and export restraints for textiles and clothing, a major distortion in the trading system for much of its his-tory, was mostly abolished in 2005 as required by the 1995 WTO Agreement on Textiles and Clothing. However, tariff barriers to trade in this sector remain high, and competitive exporters continue to confront the threat of contingent protection – safeguards and, espe-cially, antidumping. Antidumping has become a frequently used instrument in both industrialized and developing countries. In terms of the simple ratio of number of actions taken to total imports, developing countries are now the most intensive users of antidumping (Table 7.1). The majority of cases target developing countries. The existence of antidumping creates substantial uncertainty regarding the conditions of market access facing exporters. Investigations have a chilling effect on imports (they signal to importers to diversify away from targeted suppliers). This has been of long-standing concern to

East Asian countries in particular. China now confronts the highest incidence of investigations and the highest average level of duties in many countries, including other developing economies.

Antidumping actions may offer some comfort to import-competing interests, but they do little to encourage adjustment. Indeed, they create incentives to avoid adjustment. It is sometimes argued that contingent protection can be important as a vehicle that supports more general trade liberalization, so that the net effect may be positive. However, this does not mean AD is an efficient means of supporting liberalization. Given that the use of contingent protection is motivated by a need to adjust to import competition, putting in place mechanisms to bolster the ability of firms, workers and communities to adjust to changing market conditions is a superior policy. Here as in other areas, there is a need to use other instruments, not trade policy.

Services

The GATS is a major extension of the trading system, providing a framework to liberalize trade and agree on policy disciplines. To date, it has not generated much trade liberalization. Offers in the Doha Round were widely regarded as limited. A major challenge in negotiating international disciplines on services-related policies is to define meaningful commitments that will be beneficial to the countries that undertake them *and* be of value from a mercantilist negotiating perspective. A problem here is that the poorest countries have weak export interests in most services, and many will not be of great export interest to large players in the WTO. While they confront particularly high barriers in the one mode that is of export relevance to them – in

Table 7.1 Top 10 users of antidumping: initiations, 1995–2003

Initiating country/region	Number of cases	Share of total (%)
India	379	15.7
United States	329	13.6
EU-15	274	11.3
Argentina	180	7.5
South Africa	166	6.9
Australia	163	6.7
Canada	122	5.0
Brazil	109	4.5
Mexico	73	3.0
China	72	3.0

mode 4 – this is the mode that is least likely to be liberalized by rich countries, given the political sensitivities associated with both migration and outsourcing. Thus, most of the potential gains will come from domestic reforms, with successful liberalization often being conditional on substantial strengthening of domestic regulatory institutions and infrastructure.

These considerations suggest traditional mercantilist bargaining may not do much to improve outcomes in many of the poorest countries. Arguably additional instruments are needed that focus attention on the policies that are most detrimental. One such instrument is what has come to be called "aid for trade," see below. Such aid can help ensure that regulatory preconditions for liberalization to be beneficial are satisfied. By putting this additional instrument on the table, the GATS could become much more relevant as a mechanism to promote not just services liberalization but, more importantly, to bolster and improve domestic reform in services.

Of course, services are important for developed countries as well. OECD members continue to impose numerous restrictions on trade and investment in services. Reciprocal liberalization may be an effective mechanism for these countries to open their markets. However, it is worth pointing out that very little research has been done on the political economy of services trade and policy reforms. The political economy should differ in some dimensions – reflecting the more limited tradability of services and the fact that services will often be inputs into production – and this may imply that there is less scope to harness reciprocity to promote liberalization of services.

To date, the available, limited, evidence suggests that with the exception of the EU, most services policy reform has been unilateral. The more recent vintage PTAs have greater sectoral coverage than the GATS, but how much discipline they impose in practice, whether in terms of required legal change or in terms of actual implementation, is not known. This makes it difficult to determine if PTAs are more effective "lock-in" devices than the GATS. In many service markets the key need is to reform regulatory policies that impede contestability. Whether this can be facilitated through trade agreements is still very much an open question. Services often need some type of regulation to address market failures or achieve social (non-economic) objectives. Many of the "backbone" services that are critical for the competitiveness of firms in a country – such as transport, energy, and telecommunications – are industries with important network externalities, requiring regulation to ensure connection to the network at reasonable costs, etc. Designing and enforcing policies to achieve this is not trivial, suggesting a cautious approach towards the setting of enforceable international standards in trade agreements is justified. The implication is that mechanisms to encourage learning from experience through information collection and sharing may be more effective and useful than seeking to negotiate hard obligations.

Discriminatory trade arrangements

Preferential trade agreements have now proliferated to such an extent that pretty much all WTO Members are party to several such agreements. While reciprocal PTAs have predominantly involved developed nations, increasingly, developing countries are engaged in PTA negotiations. In part, this reflects developments on the non-reciprocal preference front. What follows first discusses issues raised by the latter.

Non-reciprocal trade preferences

As discussed above, developing countries are often granted preferential access to rich country markets through GSP programs that are covered by the Enabling Clause. There is an extensive economic literature that concludes that preferences often do little good from a development perspective and may actually do harm. Reasons for this include:[5]

- Countries benefiting from preferential access are subject to rules of origin. These may be so constraining that countries are forced to pay the MFN tariff because they cannot satisfy the requirements. Research reveals that utilization rates of preferences are often much less than 100 percent.
- Often goods in which developing countries have a comparative advantage are the most "sensitive" products that have the highest tariffs. Preferences for these products are frequently limited.
- Preferences are uncertain, subject to unilateral change or withdrawal, and to (non-trade) conditionality (labor or environmental norms, etc.).
- Preferences can generate serious trade diversion as the set of goods that beneficiary developing countries produce will tend to overlap with other developing countries that are not beneficiaries.
- Even in cases where preferences have value – that is, they apply to highly protected sectors in donor countries – the associated rents will be partly captured by importers and distributors in the high-income country.

• There is evidence suggesting that preferences are associated with higher own tariffs, which in turn impedes trade performance.

Recent preference schemes for the poorest countries such as the EU *Everything But Arms* (EBA) initiative for LDCs, the US *African Growth and Opportunity Act* (AGOA) or the January 2003 duty/quota free access program for LDCs implemented by Canada provide more meaningful preferential access than traditional GSP-type programs. For many products exported by the poorest countries, tariffs in high-income countries are now zero. However, they continue to be plagued by many of the factors summarized above.

From a systemic perspective, preferences create a challenge not just because they violate the non-discrimination principle, but because they may impede MFN liberalization. By definition, as MFN barriers are reduced, the value of any preference will be eroded. The more valuable are preferences to a country, the greater the incentive for that country to oppose multilateral, MFN liberalization. This is perhaps of greatest significance in the agricultural context, where some developing countries indirectly benefit from OECD domestic support programs because they have preferential access to a highly protected market – the EC sugar regime is an example. The result can be a "bootlegger-Baptist" implicit coalition – the preference programs create incentives for beneficiary countries to support OECD farm interests, and vice versa, for the farm lobby to argue that liberalization should be opposed because it would hurt the preferred developing country suppliers.

The diversification and development of exports were the primary motivation for preferences. Many countries in the past have benefited from preferential access and have graduated from bilateral programs, and others continue to benefit. But many of the poorest countries have not managed to use preferences to diversify and expand exports. Given the systemic downsides, limited benefits, and historical inability of many poor countries to use preferences, a decision to shift away from preferential trade as a form of aid could both improve development outcomes and help strengthen the multilateral trading system. Tariffs are just a part of the overall set of factors constraining developing country exports – other variables include transport costs, NTBs, and regulatory measures that are often more costly per unit of output than those confronting firms located in more developed countries. The same is true with respect to internal transactions and operating costs in these countries, which reduce competitiveness of firms. With or without preferences, benefiting more from integration into the trading system requires instruments aimed at improving the productivity and compctitiveness of firms and farmers in the poorest countries. This suggests that more, and more effective, development assistance that targets domestic supply constraints will have high returns.

Given the evidence that preferences have not been a very effective development tool, the solution is not to seek to maintain preference margins (and slow down or block MFN liberalization) but for donor countries to shift to more efficient and effective instruments of development assistance. One option that could be considered as an alternative to maintaining preference margins is for OECD countries to help current developing country beneficiaries adjust through direct income support-type instruments (targeted at affected farmers and firms and decoupled from past production levels). More generally, what is required is assistance to help affected countries deal with the associated adjustment costs by supporting diversification into other activities, retraining, and so forth. Numerous models and analyses document that the gains from trade reform outweigh any losses – what is needed are mechanisms that will transfer some of these gains into the financing needed to provide such assistance.

Reciprocal PTAs

The growth of reciprocal PTAs has been significant in recent years. While motivations are multidimensional, a desire to obtain more secure access to major markets, and/or a fear of being left out while the rest of the world signs PTAs are often part of the equation. As secure and liberal access is something that should be provided by the WTO, the proliferation of PTAs is a symptom of a failure of the WTO to perform its function. A proliferation of PTAs motivated by discriminatory or insurance objectives can only be detrimental to the majority of developing countries that will be left out of PTAs for political or other reasons. By reducing trade barriers for a subset of partners, countries generally increase the real cost of their imports, reduce the flow of technology from non-Member countries and increase dependence on particular export markets. They may also make it more difficult to reduce barriers against non-preferred imports in the future. Trade diversion caused by PTAs may worsen excluded countries' terms of trade as non-Member suppliers become less competitive because they continue to pay tariffs while competing producers from Member countries do not.

Increasingly PTAs are covering issues that have proven divisive in the WTO, such as investment, labor, environment, or competition policies. Recent examples are the US–Central America Free Trade

Agreement and the European Union's ongoing effort to negotiate Economic Partnership Agreements with ACP countries. This raises a serious potential concern insofar as these countries perceive disciplines in such areas as not being in their interest but the price required for guaranteed access. Clearly, much depends on the coverage of agreements and in particular whether the regulatory disciplines for "behind the border" policies are appropriate in the sense that the benefits outweigh the costs of implementation. The WTO has an important role to play in reducing the magnitude of PTA-created discrimination in trade through its periodic rounds of trade negotiations. In addition, WTO Members should focus more energy on monitoring of PTAs *ex post* (What do they do? What are their effects?) as opposed to primarily undertaking an *ex ante* assessment that centers on the legal obligations of Members and that rarely comes to a definite conclusion.[6]

Three specific changes would arguably make North–South PTAs – which are rapidly proliferating and are often promoted on development grounds – more "development friendly": (1) unconditional acceptance by all parties to MFN – not preferential – liberalization of trade in goods and services by the developing country signatories; (2) building mechanisms to pursue priority national regulatory policy objectives in developing country partners as opposed to harmonization on the standards of OECD countries, while maintaining the role of PTAs as a commitment device; and (3) strengthened grant-based financing mechanisms to improve trade supply capacity and increase the benefits of trade reforms based on a local analysis of needs, with allocations determined by the country's overall development strategy. The first item, MFN liberalization *by the developing countries,* would not imply a requirement to move to zero tariffs across the board – instead the goal would be a significant reduction in applied MFN tariffs by developing country partners, bound in the WTO. This would prevent trade diversion, reduce the administrative burden on customs authorities (as there is no need for rules of origin to be enforced on imports), help ensure that the PTA benefits all trading partners, not just Members, and allow governments more time to put in place alternative sources of fiscal revenue. This proposal will require a change in Art. XXIV GATT and Art. V. GATS, or waivers for the PTAs that adopt this proposal.

Institutional challenges

Several systemic challenges emerged in the first ten years of the WTO's operation that require resolution if the institution is to continue to

thrive. They include the development releva
disciplines, the organization of negotiation
procedures.

Development: policy coherence and aid for tra

As noted before, the focus in the GATT/   l
policies. A consequence is that trade policy   o
much. In particular, there are obvious tensi   n
(negotiating greater market access) and   :r
objectives – be it raising revenue, establishin   r
enhancing food security in rural areas. The   en
be attained more efficiently through non-tr   er,
to implement WTO disciplines, governm   ate
resources to do so, resources they may n   gher
returns if used for other purposes. Develop   one
instrument to promote the use of non-t   both
trade and non-trade objectives.

An increase in aid for trade is particu   poorest
countries as trade capacity (competitiv..... is the binding constraint.[7] In undertaking trade reform and to participate effectively in
the global trading system, poorer countries are faced with a gamut of
economic and political challenges. On the economic side, adjustment
costs will arise before offsetting investments are realized in other (new)
sectors. Preference erosion is just one element of these costs. Some
countries may confront deterioration in their terms of trade (e.g. some
net food importers). In others, tariff revenues may make up a significant proportion of total fiscal resources and they will need to
undertake tax reform. Many of the poorest developing countries are ill
equipped to take full advantage of new and existing trade opportunities due to supply-side, administrative capacity and institutional
constraints. Improved market access without the ability to supply
export markets competitively is not much use. Gains from trade liberalization are conditional on an environment that allows the mobility
of labor and capital to occur, that facilitates investment in new sectors
of activity – requiring, among other factors, an efficient financial
system, and good transportation/logistics services. Inevitably for most
poor countries this requires complementary reforms prior to and in
conjunction with the trade reforms.

On the political side, even accepting that trade is likely to generate
global gains, the distributive and re-distributive dimensions of trade
integration need to be taken into account if the political viability of

the process is to be assured. Providing sizeable assistance has historically been of considerable importance in helping persuade countries of the benefits of integration. It played a significant role in building support for the liberalization measures undertaken as part of the creation of the European Economic Community. The post-war Marshall Plan was instigated in large measure to facilitate global economic recovery by, among other things, neutralizing the forces moving Western Europe away from multilateral trade.

Trade reform undertaken in conjunction with concomitant "behind the border" policy measures and investments has significant potential to generate additional trade opportunities that would help lift a large number of people out of poverty. If complemented by actions to redistribute some of the global gains from liberalization to help address trade and growth agendas in the poorest countries, the likelihood of realizing the potential gains would increase significantly.[8]

The first step towards integrating development assistance into the WTO process was the Integrated Framework for Trade-related Technical Assistance. Created in 1997 and revamped in 2000, this program is limited to the LDCs. It brings together six multilateral agencies working on trade development issues – the IMF, the International Trade Centre, UNCTAD, the UN Development Programme, WTO and the World Bank – and over a dozen bilateral donors. The basic purpose is to embed a trade agenda into a country's overall development strategy, starting with a diagnostic analysis of the prevailing trade constraints that informs a proposed action matrix of trade-related capacity building and assistance. While the Integrated Framework reduces the duplication and proliferation of trade initiatives and helps ensure that assistance is provided according to the needs identified by the country, it does not guarantee that trade needs will be financed as trade interventions and investments must compete with other sectors such as health and education.

The operationalization of aid for trade is still a work in progress. In mid-2006 a decision was taken to establish an independent secretariat to manage the Integrated Framework, and to greatly increase its funding (to a proposed $400 million). As far as non-LDCs are concerned, a WTO Aid for Trade Task Force was established in February 2006 pursuant to the Hong Kong Ministerial Declaration. It was asked to deliberate on the scope of aid for trade, how it related to the WTO in supporting the development dimensions of the Doha Round, and to identify appropriate delivery mechanisms. The taskforce made a series of recommendations in its July 2006 report, one of which was to establish a monitoring body in the WTO that would undertake a periodic global review based on information from the countries concerned, donors and international organizations. It also proposed that an assessment of aid for trade – for donors and recipients – be included in WTO Trade Policy Reviews. If implemented and elaborated in cooperation with development agencies that are active in developing countries, these recommendations could help move the WTO towards helping countries to achieve their growth objectives with less reliance on trade policy.

Policy space

The Doha Round (the "Doha Development Agenda") put development concerns much more centrally in WTO deliberations than ever before. This helps to explain the rise in prominence of development assistance-related matters in WTO discussions, and the great increase in funding for WTO technical assistance noted in Chapter 2. However, the WTO can do little more than advocate for more assistance to be given to the trade area – ultimately allocation decisions are (and must be) taken by developing country governments. And, as stated before, there is only so much trade policy can do to promote development. Clearly poverty reduction and economic growth prospects would be enhanced by the agenda summarized previously: a substantial reduction in MFN tariffs, especially tariff peaks in textiles and agriculture (in the process, attenuating trade diversion effects of PTAs), elimination of agricultural export subsidies and decoupling of domestic subsidies, stronger disciplines on antidumping, and giving more attention to establishing well-regulated, internationally-contestable service markets.

What about WTO rules? Developing countries have historically played only a minor role in the multilateral trading system. Until the Uruguay Round, their participation was *à la carte*. Many did not make commitments. This changed with the entry into force of the WTO in 1995. Because of the so-called Single Undertaking, developing countries became subject to almost all the disciplines of the many agreements contained in the WTO (after transition periods expired). Some of these agreements, in particular TRIPs, were skewed towards benefiting rich countries. TRIPs and other agreements generated asymmetric implementation costs, as the rules reflected existing practices in OECD countries. As a result, it is not too much of an exaggeration to speak of a Uruguay Round "hangover" for many developing countries – and a great deal of skepticism regarding the benefits of WTO membership.[9]

Many developing countries are now actively seeking to improve their "terms of trade" in the WTO. Examples are the formation of the G-20 group of developing countries in the run-up to the 2003 Ministerial meeting in Cancún and the formation of a West African coalition with a focus on cotton subsidies. The G-20 included Brazil, China, India and South Africa and operated as a coalition in Cancún.[10] West African countries – Benin, Burkina Faso, Chad and Niger – sought the abolition of export and other trade-distorting subsidies granted to cotton producers in the US, the EU and China, and that their cotton farmers be compensated during a proposed three-year transition period during which subsidies were to be phased out.

Such active engagement is clearly a precondition for defending national interests. In the above cases these interests revolve around market access and trade-distorting practices. More challenging is what approach to take to deal with rule making from a development perspective. Historically, development issues have been dealt with in the WTO through SDT and/or transition periods. While low-income countries with weak institutional capacity simply may not be able to benefit much from implementing certain WTO agreements, the approach has not created a strong sense of "ownership" of WTO agreements. Indeed, from an economic perspective, the WTO approach of allowing the poorest countries the greatest leeway to use trade policies is arguably not helping to improve economic development prospects.

Rather than simply exempting (some) developing countries from WTO rules, a new framework for SDT could be considered that would more actively support development prospects of poor countries as opposed to effectively encouraging them to use (ineffective) trade instruments. This framework would place greater emphasis on dialogue, exchange of information, and multilateral monitoring and assessment of the impact of policies and the extent to which developing countries are granted assistance in the trade area. There is an important link here with the broader issue of policy coherence, both between trade and aid policies in the North, and, as critical, between the regional trade agreement strategies pursued by rich countries in the context of negotiations with developing countries and the approach taken in the WTO towards "behind the border" issues. From a development perspective, what matters is that trade-related policy disciplines make economic sense.

Several options have been proposed in the literature to go beyond the current approach towards SDT:

- Allow "policy flexibility" for all developing countries as currently (self-) defined in the WTO in terms of whether to implement a specific set of (new) rules, as long as this does not impose significant negative spillovers on other Members.[11]
- Adopt a country-specific approach that would make implementation of new rules a function of national priorities. WTO disciplines implying significant resources would be implemented only when this conforms with or supports the attainment of national development strategies. A process of multilateral monitoring and surveillance, with input by international development agencies, would be established to ensure that decisions are subject to scrutiny and debate.
- Adopt an agreement-specific approach involving the *ex ante* setting of specific criteria on an agreement-by-agreement basis to determine whether a country could opt out of applying negotiated disciplines for a limited time period. Criteria could include indicators of administrative capacity, country size and level of development, and a link might be made between implementation and the provision of financial and technical assistance.
- A simple rule-of-thumb approach that would allow opt-outs for resource-intensive agreements for all countries satisfying broad threshold criteria such as minimum level of per capita income, institutional capacity, or economic scale. The presumption here is that this would allow the bulk of identified difficulties to be tackled at little or no negotiating cost. The criteria would apply to *all* new resource-intensive agreements. Invocation of an opt-out would be voluntary. As countries come to surpass thresholds over time, disciplines automatically would become applicable.

A common element of such proposals is that use is made of economic criteria to determine their scope. This is rather controversial in the WTO as greater explicit differentiation among countries is rejected by many developing country representatives. Currently, whether a rule is enforced is left to individual Members (i.e., whether or not to self-declare as a developing country) and a mix of unilateral action and bargaining by developed country Members whether to accept this and whether to provide SDT. Country classification inevitably creates tensions among governments as to which countries would be eligible. The advantage of simple criteria is that it is "clean" – there is no need for additional negotiation. The disadvantage is that criteria inherently will be somewhat arbitrary.

Movement towards a rule- or agreement-specific set of criteria has proven feasible in the past – witness the SCM Agreement per capita

income threshold for the use of export subsidies, the net food importers group defined in the Uruguay Round, or the group of countries
that do not have a pharmaceutical industry that were the focal point
of the Doha Round TRIPS/public health debate. However, this type of
approach does little to engage governments and stakeholders, or help
them identify better policies and areas where complementary actions/
investments are needed. Instead it is driven by a desire to carve out
"space" to avoid being confronted with a dispute.

An alternative would be to move towards greater use of a soft law
approach for new, "behind the border" issues – including sensitive
policy areas such as labor and competition law or the regulation of
genetically modified organisms – issues that have proven to be very
controversial, in part because of great uncertainty regarding the
repercussions of international rules. Soft law involves establishment of
a framework for international cooperation on issues. It relies on
mechanisms to encourage learning through regular interactions of
relevant policy-makers and constituents (stakeholders), peer review,
and (multilateral) monitoring of the impacts of policies and their
effectiveness in attaining stated objectives. From an economic perspective, depending on the issue, a soft law approach instead of efforts
to impose specific "good practices" may make good sense.[12]

A premise that underlies arguments for soft law (be it implicit or
explicit) is that the mechanism of reciprocity may be inappropriate to
define common rules for "behind the border" regulatory policies. The
specific content of regulation should reflect national (or local) circumstances. A framework for assisting governments to identify good
policies, not a system that aims at harmonization enforced by binding
dispute settlement and decisions by a small set of judges, may be most
appropriate from an economic welfare and a democratic accountability perspective. This could also allow a more considered and flexible approach towards determining at what level eventual binding
international cooperation should occur – bilateral, regional, or multilateral. Perhaps most important, greater policy dialogue and multilateral monitoring of the effects of policies applied by WTO Members
could both help to increase the (domestic) accountability of governments and the "ownership" of policies and the multilateral rules that
(eventually) are agreed to apply to specific policies. Greater transparency is critical to prevent capture of policies by interest groups, to
make policies contestable and to give both winners and losers a
greater voice in policy formation.

Summing up, when it comes to rules (especially the non-market
access, "behind the border" agenda), there is a basic choice to be

made between the pursuit of universal rules that in principle apply to all Members, and that will by necessity require SDT provisions to account for country differences, and a plurilateral approach without SDT. The latter appears to be an attractive way of allowing a subset of the membership to move forward in the absence of consensus. However, many developing countries are on record in the WTO as opposing moves towards greater use of such agreements, primarily on the basis of resistance to the creation of a multi-tier trading system. Such an approach also does little to help promote development. A recast framework for SDT could do much to make plurilateral agreements redundant by both facilitating new rule making *and* improving the substance of disciplines from a development perspective.

Negotiating processes and decision-making procedures

In the post-Seattle period questions were raised regarding the governance and procedures of the WTO. The 1999 Ministerial meeting in Seattle and the 2003 meeting in Cancún illustrated that meetings of trade ministers may do little to advance discussions or to generate decisions in the absence of a clear agenda and clear options. Members entered the Cancún Ministerial divided on agricultural and non-agricultural negotiating modalities, on whether to launch negotiations on the so-called Singapore issues and their possible scope, on the approach to take towards strengthening existing WTO provisions on SDT for developing countries and how to address implementation problems left over from the Uruguay Round. In the period following the 2001 Doha Ministerial, most deadlines were missed, sometimes repeatedly. Only one of the major issues of concern to developing countries was settled before Cancún – the TRIPS and public health decision summarized above – and then only after long delay and rancorous negotiation.

While there are obviously substantive differences in views on all these issues, the question of how agendas are set and whether the consensus rule should be revisited may need to be discussed. Numerous observers both in and outside of government have questioned the governance and procedures of the WTO. Consensus is both a major strength and a weakness of the WTO. It is obviously difficult and cumbersome to negotiate among 150 countries. Moves towards the creation of negotiating coalitions of groups of countries may reduce the number of "principals" but possibly at the cost of greater inflexibility and a need for more time to consult. Here there is an implication for the organization of Ministerials, as Ministers will not have the time needed to engage in lengthy consultations within and across coalitions. This suggests that the Geneva process should be strengthened, Ministerial meetings be better prepared – and perhaps remain limited to Geneva, where the infrastructure is in place, and there must be greater flexibility in terms of the timing (periodicity) of Ministerials.

Many proposals have been made to change the governance structure of the WTO. Proposals to move away from consensus and create a decision-making and management structure that relies on an Executive Board or Committee of the type found in the World Bank or the IMF have been made for many years. A move in this direction would imply that certain WTO Members would speak on behalf of those they were chosen to represent – this is the World Bank or the IMF model. An alternative, less ambitious change would be to give such a committee the task of hammering out a proposed consensus on issues, which would then need to be ratified by all WTO Members – in effect, formalizing the Green room process.

Many developing countries object strongly to the IMF or World Bank model, as they believe that the consensus principle maximizes their ability to safeguard their interests. Rather than pursue major structural reforms, they proposed instead that the focus be on procedural improvements to ensure that small group meetings (such as the Green room) are transparent. This could involve agreeing that consultations be open-ended, that all Members are informed that Green room meetings are being pursued, that all Members be given an opportunity to state their views, and that the outcome is reported in a timely fashion to those WTO Members not present. Much was done post-Seattle to make the Green room process more transparent, although this comes at the inevitable cost of requiring more time to inform all stakeholders of the state of play – a factor that is especially important in bringing a Ministerial meeting to a successful conclusion, as time will be in short supply.

A related question concerns access by civil society (NGOs) to WTO deliberations. NGOs have noted repeatedly that they can obtain observer status at UN meetings, but are excluded from the WTO. This exclusion pertains not just to sensitive negotiation and dispute settlement sessions, but also to regular committee and Council meetings. We are of the view that greater access can do harm and may do much good. What matters most is accountability *ex post* of policy-makers and greater transparency of WTO meetings could help achieve that. Such access should not extend to be able to participate – as the WTO is a governmental body – nor does it have to be physical. Given the Internet and the low cost of telecom services, every regular WTO meeting could be taped and web cast.

Many NGOs are also eager to obtain access to panels in order to defend environmental and other interests. The Appellate Body has taken the decision to accept amicus briefs. Going further and allowing observers to monitor panel proceedings would require changes in the dispute settlement mechanism – including probably the professionalization of panels. Whatever may be decided in terms of public access to deliberations, there are very good arguments against granting private parties standing to take cases to the WTO. The WTO is an intergovernmental body where the premise is that it is up to national governments to determine and defend the balance of rights and obligations.

Transparency: towards greater monitoring and evaluation

Greater transparency of policy – not just identification of the existence of policies, but assessments of their effects – was mentioned several times in the foregoing. More frequent and more in-depth analysis of trade policies in WTO Members, of the impacts of PTAs, and of the extent to which high-income countries have responded with assistance to address priorities that were identified by developing countries would do much to support more constructive engagement of business and NGOs with the WTO. A more economically informed "constituency" might enhance the quality of interaction between WTO Members in instances where countries are not in conformity with a negotiated set of WTO rules. Greater multilateral monitoring of the actions of developing and developed countries would allow greater scope to both safeguard/enhance market access *and* enhance the development relevance of the WTO.

Services offer an example of the potential for the WTO to become a more effective mechanism to assist governments in identifying and addressing the domestic reform agenda. If WTO Members were to expand the transparency mandate of the organization to make the WTO a focal point for multilateral discussions and assessments of the state of Members' service sectors, the institution could do much to help address the needs of its poorer Members by raising the policy profile of the services agenda in these countries and identifying where investments/assistance are needed. By combining its commitment and monitoring "technologies" to mobilize liberalization commitments that are conditional on assistance, and monitoring the delivery and effectiveness of such assistance, the WTO could play a useful role in both helping Members and expanding the coverage of its agreements.

More effective monitoring of the implementation of PTAs and assessments of their impacts on non-Members would also be beneficial. As mentioned above, the primary mechanism offered by the WTO to reduce trade diversion costs for non-PTA Members is through negotiating rounds. The more information both Members and non-Members have on the effects of PTAs, the greater the prospect of such negotiations being constructive.

Greater efforts to ensure transparency do not necessarily have to involve the WTO itself. Another option that can be considered is the creation of a set of regional research and public interest bodies that would be tasked with monitoring of policies at the country level, assess their impacts, etc. Such entities could also explore the economic and social aspects of specific contentious issues or proposed areas for action at the WTO or in a PTA context. Such transparency bodies can help shed light and build consensus by identifying whether there are cross-border spillovers, their size, the economic or environmental impact of policies, including their distributional effects within and across countries, and whether alternative instruments exist that could attain governmental or societal objectives (more) efficiently.

Concluding remarks

Much is demanded of the WTO by a wide variety of interests. It is important that the organization not be asked to do too much. While the WTO should not lose sight of its trade focus, it can, with a few adjustments, do much more to assist its poorer Members in attaining their development objectives, and in bolstering support for the trading system in its Members. The measures proposed here are premised on the view that the core mandate of the WTO revolves around trade and trade liberalization – that is, reducing discrimination between national and foreign goods and services, and between different foreign suppliers of similar products. In this context, we believe that increased transparency through greater multilateral monitoring and "surveillance" can do much to hold all Members accountable for their performance on trade policy and the delivery of development assistance promises.

Glossary

Actionable subsidy. A type of subsidy that is not prohibited under WTO rules but against which a Member may respond by imposing a countervailing duty.

Ad valorem. An ad valorem duty (tariff, charge, and so on) is based on the value of the dutiable item and expressed in percentage terms, for example, 10 percent of the assessed value.

Antidumping. Measures imposed by importing governments to counteract dumping, for example by imposing duties or negotiating price increases. May be calculated as the margin of dumping or limited to the level of injury imposed by dumping if this is less than the dumping margin.

Codex Alimentarius. An international set of standards, codes of practice, and guidelines and recommendations relating to food quality and safety, including codes governing hygienic processing practices, recommendations relating to compliance with standards, limits for pesticide residues, and guidelines for contaminants, food additives, and veterinary drugs. The Codex Alimentarius Commission is the body responsible for compiling the standards.

Contingent protection. Trade barriers that are imposed if certain circumstances (contingencies) are met. Examples include antidumping or countervailing duties (to offset subsidies) and safeguards. Also called administered protection.

Countervailing duty. Tariff levied on imports of goods that have benefited from production or export subsidies. The duty is intended to offset the effect of the subsidy.

Customs union. A group of countries forming a single customs territory in which: (1) tariffs and other barriers are eliminated on substantially all the trade between the constituent countries for products originating in these countries; and (2) there is a common external trade policy (common external tariff) that applies to non-Members.

Customs valuation. Establishment, according to defined criteria, of the value of goods for the purpose of levying ad valorem customs duties on their importation.

Dispute Settlement Body. WTO body that is responsible for dealing with disputes between WTO Members. Consists of all WTO Members meeting together to consider the reports of dispute settlement panels and the Appellate Body.

Dumping. A form of price discrimination by which the export price of the product exported from one country to another is less than the comparable price, in the ordinary course of trade – that is, including transport and related costs – for the like product when destined for consumption in the exporting country (Art. VI GATT). Also defined as sales below the estimated cost of production. The margin of dumping is the difference between the two prices.

Duty drawback. A duty drawback scheme is a form of border tax adjustment whereby the duties or taxes levied on imported goods are refunded, in whole or in part, when the goods are re-exported. The idea is to reduce the burden on exporters while maintaining tariffs for revenue or protective purposes.

Economic needs test. Measure requiring a demonstration that an import (of goods but more usually natural service providers) cannot be satisfied by local producers or service providers.

Enabling Clause. A 1971 GATT Decision on "Differential and More Favorable Treatment, Reciprocity and Fuller Participation of Developing Countries." One of the so-called Framework agreements, it enables WTO Members, notwithstanding the non-discrimination requirements, to "accord differential and more favorable treatment to developing countries, without according such treatment to other contracting parties."

Exhaustion. Legal regime pertaining to imports of goods protected under intellectual property rights. Under national exhaustion, rights end upon the first sale of the good within a nation, and right holders may prevent unauthorized imports of the goods concerned. Under international exhaustion, rights end upon the first sale anywhere in the world, after which parallel imports are permitted.

Externality. Occurs when the action of one agent (person, firm, government) directly affects other agents, making them better or worse off. Beneficial effects are called positive externalities; harmful ones negative externalities.

Fast track. A procedure under which the US Congress agrees to consider implementing legislation for international trade agreements on an "up or down" basis, that is, gives up its right to propose amendments. Now called Trade promotion authority.

Free riding. Situation in which a country does not contribute to a specific agreement or commit to apply specific disciplines while still benefiting from the commitments made by other countries or parties to the agreement.

Free trade area. A group of countries in which the tariffs and other barriers are eliminated on substantially all trade between them. Each member maintains its own external trade policy against nonmembers. Also called free trade agreement or free trade arrangement.

Generalized System of Preferences (GSP). A system through which industrialized countries grant preferential access to their markets to developing countries.

Geographical indication. Measure intended to protect the reputation for quality of goods originating in a particular geographic location by limiting the use of distinctive place names or regional appellations to goods actually produced in those locations.

Green room. Used to describe discussions in the WTO among a subset of countries, generally the major OECD members and a small number of developing countries.

Least developed country (LDC). A country that satisfies a number of criteria established by the United Nations that together imply a very low level of economic development. As of 2002, the UN had classified 49 countries in the LDC group.

Mode of supply. Term used in the GATS context to identify how a service is provided by a supplier to a buyer.

Most favored nation (MFN). Core principle of the WTO. MFN is the "normal," non-discriminatory tariff charged on imports of a good. In commercial diplomacy, exporters seek MFN treatment that is, the promise that they will be treated as well as the most favored exporter.

Mutual recognition. The acceptance by one country of another country's certification that a product has satisfied a product standard. Often based on formal agreements between countries if the standards are mandatory.

National treatment. Principle that foreign goods, services, and persons (investors), once they have entered a country and satisfied any formalities that are required, are treated in exactly the same way as national goods, services, or persons. In particular, they face the same internal taxes and no additional restrictions.

Nontariff barrier (NTB). A catchall phrase describing barriers to international trade other than tariffs, for example, quotas or licensing requirements.

Nonviolation. Procedure under WTO dispute settlement provisions under which a WTO Member argues that actions by another Member, even though allowed under WTO rules, nullify or impair benefits expected under the agreement.

Phytosanitary regulation. Pertaining to the health of plants. *See* SPS measure.

Protocol of accession. Legal document recording the conditions and obligations under which a country accedes to an international agreement or organization.

Quid pro quo. Used to describe the counterpart offer that must be offered by a Member in order to obtain a concession from another Member.

Reciprocity. Fundamental principle of WTO negotiations requiring that there be a balance in the exchange of concessions undertaken by WTO Members. The way this balance is to be determined may be defined before the negotiations start, e.g., the value of tariff revenue collected (lost), the value of trade flows affected, the average change in the tariffs of goods that are liberalized, etc.

Request offer. Negotiating procedure based on the tabling, by each party, of a list of concessions requested of other parties, followed by an offer list of the concessions that could be granted if its request were met.

Remedy. Legal term to describe a measure recommended by a WTO dispute settlement panel that aims to bring the policies of a Member found to have violated WTO rules or disciplines into compliance with its obligations.

Retaliation. Imposition of a trade barrier in response to another country's increasing its level of trade restrictions.

Rule of origin. Criterion for establishing the country of origin of a product. Often based on whether production (processing) leads to a change in tariff heading (classification) or on the level of value added in the country where the good was last processed.

Safeguard. Clause in a legal text allowing temporary derogation from its provisions under certain specified emergency conditions.

Safeguard action. Emergency protection to safeguard domestic producers of a specific good from an unforeseen surge in imports (Art. XIX GATT), to protect a country's external financial position and balance of payments (Art. XII, XVIII.B GATT), or to protect an infant industry in a developing country (Art. XVIII.A or C GATT).

Sanitary and phytosanitary (SPS) measure. A technical requirement specifying criteria to ensure food safety and animal and plant health. Many international SPS standards are set by the Codex Alimentarius Commission.

Special and differential treatment. The principle that developing countries be accorded special privileges, either exempting them from some WTO rules or granting them preferential treatment in the application of WTO rules. Permitted under the Enabling Clause.

Specific tariff. A specific duty (tariff, import tax) expressed in terms of a fixed amount per unit of the dutiable item. For example, $1,000 on each imported vehicle or $50 on each ton of wheat.

Tariff binding. In the GATT context, commitment by countries not to raise particular tariff items above a specific or bound level. Also referred to as ceiling bindings. The so-called schedule of tariff concessions of each WTO Member is annexed to its protocol of accession.

Tariff equivalent. Measure of the protective effect of a NTB – the tariff that would have the exact same effect on imports as the NTB.

Tariff escalation. Occurs if the tariff increases as a good becomes more processed. Escalation discourages imports of more processed varieties of the good (discouraging foreign processing activity) and offers domestic processors positive levels of effective protection. For example, low duties on tomatoes, higher duties on tomato paste, and yet higher duties on tomato ketchup.

Tariff peaks. Tariffs that are particularly high, often defined as rates that exceed 15 percent or the average nominal tariff by a factor of more than three.

Tariff rate quota (TRQ). Measure under which a good is subject to a MFN tariff, but a certain quantity (the "quota") is admitted at a lower, sometimes zero, tariff. TRQs are mainly applied to agricultural trade and can be seasonal.

Tariffication. Procedure of converting NTBs into (equivalent) tariffs. In the Uruguay Round, all countries' agricultural NTBs were tariffed and bound.

Technical barrier to trade. Trade-restrictive effect arising from the application of technical regulations or standards such as testing requirements, labeling requirements, packaging requirements, marketing standards, certification requirements, origin-marking requirements, and health and safety regulations.

Notes

Foreword

1 See Fatoumata Jawara and Aileen Kwa, *Behind the Scenes at the WTO: The Real World of International Trade Negotiations* (London: Zed Books, 2003); and Amrita Narlikar and Rorden Wilkinson, "Collapse at the WTO: A Cancún Post-Mortem," *Third World Quarterly* 25, no. 3 (2004): 447–60.
2 See Rorden Wilkinson, *The WTO: Crisis and the Governance of Global Trade* (London: Routledge, 2006), Chapter 2, also Chapters 3–5.
3 See John S. Odell, "The Seattle Impasse and its Implications for the WTO," in Daniel Kennedy and James Southwick (eds) *The Political Economy of International Trade Law: Essays in Honor of Robert Hudec* (Cambridge: Cambridge University Press, 2002), 400–29; and John S. Odell, "Chairing a WTO Negotiation," *Journal of International Economic Law* 8, no. 2 (2005): 425–88.
4 Bernard Hoekman and Michel Kostecki, *The Political Economy of the World Trading System* (Oxford: Oxford University Press, 1995, and 2nd edn 2001).

Introduction

1 A classic illustration is a statement attributed to a GATT representative in addressing the Director-General during the Uruguay Round: "Sir, there is a difference between you and me; I am a Contracting Party [to the GATT] and you are a Contracted Party." Nothing changed with the creation of the WTO.
2 Horn and Mavroidis have published a comprehensive WTO dispute settlement dataset. See Henrik Horn and Petros C. Mavroidis, "WTO Dispute Settlement Database" (2006), http://www.worldbank.org/trade/wtodisputes.
3 See John H. Jackson, *Sovereignty, the WTO, and Changing Fundamentals of International Law* (Cambridge: Cambridge University Press, 2006).

1 A brief history of the world trading system

1 The material in this and the next chapter draws in part on Bernard M. Hoekman and Michel Kostecki, *The Political Economy of the World Trading*

System (Oxford: Oxford University Press, 2001), Chapters 1 and 2, and in part on Petros C. Mavroidis, *The GATT: A Commentary* (Oxford: Oxford University Press, 2005).

2 The founding parties to the GATT were Australia, Belgium, Brazil, Burma, Canada, Ceylon, Chile, China, Cuba, Czechoslovakia, France, India, Lebanon, Luxembourg, the Netherlands, New Zealand, Norway, Pakistan, Southern Rhodesia, South Africa, Syria, the United Kingdom and the United States. China, Lebanon and Syria subsequently withdrew.

3 The highest organ in the GATT was the CONTRACTING PARTIES referring to the entire GATT membership adopting decisions by consensus.

4 The PRC never acknowledged the legitimacy of this action. Its own (i.e., reduced) participation to the GATT was left in limbo as a result. This is why, when negotiations to clarify the status of the PRC under the GATT began again in the 1980s, the Working Party established to this effect (in 1987) carried the title *"People's Republic of China's Status as a Contracting Party."*

2 The WTO in a nutshell

1 The extent of trade liberalization may and does vary across countries.

2 See Fabio Spadi, "Discriminatory Safeguards in the Light of the Admission of the People's Republic of China to the World Trade Organization," *Journal of International Economic Law* 5, no. 2 (2002): 421–43. This is a case of a WTO *plus* obligation.

3 See the discussion in Henrik Horn and Petros C. Mavroidis, "WTO Dispute Settlement Database" (2006), http://www.worldbank.org/trade/wto-disputes.

4 Donald H. Regan, "What Are Trade Agreements for?" *Journal of International Economic Law*, 9(4) (2006): 951–88.

5 Because the initial set of contracting parties to the GATT was quite small (only 23 countries), the benchmark for MFN is the best treatment offered to any country, including countries that may not be a member of the GATT/WTO.

6 See e.g., Kyle Bagwell and Robert W. Staiger, *The Economics of the World Trading System* (Cambridge, MA: MIT Press, 2003) and Wilfred J. Ethier, "Political Externalities, Nondiscrimination and a Multilateral World," *Review of International Economics* 12, no. 3 (2004): 303–20, for complementary analyses.

7 Michael Finger, "Trade Liberalization: A Public Choice Perspective," in Richard Amacher, Gottfried Haberler, and Thomas Willett (eds) *Challenges to a Liberal International Economic Order* (Washington, DC: American Enterprise Institute, 1979).

8 Case law has conferred the legal status of an exception to a basic obligation to some state contingencies, with a corresponding shift in the burden of proof.

9 In the case of the EU (a fully fledged common market with a common external trade policy), member states are represented in the WTO by the Commission of the European Communities. The practice that has evolved is that individual member states do not speak in WTO meetings on issues where the Commission has exclusive competence – such as trade policy.

10 The Director-General, the head of the WTO Secretariat, has virtually no real authority. His or her job is to run the secretariat and to act as the guardian of the collective interest of the member states. The WTO rules and procedures allow the Director-General to act as a broker or intermediary – not a decision-maker.

11 One implication of this, for example, is that WTO Secretariat members are prohibited from interpreting the WTO agreements or providing a judgment whether an existing or proposed law is WTO legal. This is something for WTO Members to decide.

12 The Swiss formula is defined as $T = MX/(M + X)$, where X is the initial tariff binding on a product; M is the maximum tariff that may be applied, and T the resulting tariff binding for the product.

13 That said, given the one Member-one vote rule, if voting were to occur, the EU would dominate with 25 votes.

3 The GATT

1 In the context of the panel proceedings on *Japan – Alcoholic Beverages II*, the Appellate Body (AB) held decisions by the GATT CONTRACTING PARTIES to adopt panel reports do not form part of the GATT legal *acquis* (§ 115). Hence, although case law has exercised a considerable influence on the shaping of the GATT/WTO law, it is not *formally* part of the GATT 1994.

2 In our discussion of the legal disciplines, we make use of panel and Appellate Body reports both to illustrate the key provisions to give a flavor of the process through which the rules are interpreted and clarified. Readers seeking an introduction to the economics of the WTO are referred to Bernard M. Hoekman and Michel Kostecki, *The Political Economy of the World Trading System* (Oxford: Oxford University Press, 2001). This work also contains comprehensive references to the more specialized literature.

3 Export subsidies as well are a border measure. We treat them however, along with domestic subsidies since their treatment comes under the same agreement.

4 Recently, the AB in *EC – Chicken Cuts* concluded that the HS provides the legal context for the interpretation of the GATT. This means that WTO panels/AB are now required to examine the HS (and its rules for interpretation) in order to adjudicate disputes relating to the interpretation (ambit) of a concession.

5 The WTO Agreement on Rules of Origin does little to help here – it is essentially a framework for future negotiations. WTO Members are only required to apply their unilaterally defined rules of origin in a non-discriminatory manner.

6 The term *like products* has a completely different meaning in the context of Art. III GATT, the national treatment obligation, see below.

7 The convention in WTO disputes is to name only the defendant followed by a short description of the product concerned.

8 See *EC – Bananas III* (WTO/DS27/R/MEX) (§ 7.239). This test is of course highly subjective and almost impossible to verify. To argue that it is because of a particular measure that competitive opportunities have been

affected, an analysis of effects and their possible causes would be needed. That this is not done reflects the lack of influence economic analysis has in GATT/WTO dispute settlement adjudication.

9 On the interpretation of the term "ordinary customs duties," see pp. 96ff. of the Appellate Body report on *Chile – Price Band System*.

10 There is still substantial confusion as to what exactly constitutes an "other duty or charge" and where the boundary is with ordinary customs duties. Case law has provided some clarification: both types can be negotiated and be bound (Petros C. Mavroidis, *The GATT: A Commentary* (Oxford: Oxford University Press, 2005), 56–71).

11 However, in the context of the Enabling Clause, the AB accepted that, to the extent that *objective* criteria have been used, a Member may condition additional benefits to its trading partners on their satisfaction. It remains to be seen if this case law will be "exported" to an Art. I GATT analysis.

12 The GATT/WTO also contains another instrument with potentially an even wider reach: the non-violation instrument. This allows a Member to argue that a policy of another Member, even though legal (unconstrained by WTO) has adverse effects. This has not had much of an impact (seen much use) as no effective remedy is available given that by definition the measures concerned are legal.

13 See Stephen Weatherill, "Pre-emption, Harmonisation and the Distribution of Competence to Regulate the Internal Market," in Catherine Barnard and Joanne Scott (eds) *The Law of the Single European Market* (Oxford: Hart Publishing, 2002), 41–73.

14 See Bernard M. Hoekman and Petros C. Mavroidis (eds) *Law and Policy in Public Purchasing* (Michigan: University of Michigan Press, 1997).

15 As mentioned, the terminology used in Art. III GATT dealing with fiscal (§ 2) and non-fiscal measures (§ 4) is not the same. Whereas the former refers to both like and directly competitive or substitutable products as the category of products which will serve as basis to establish comparability of treatment, the latter refers to like products only. In *EC – Asbestos* the AB clarified that the two provisions are co-extensive, in that the term "like" in Art. III.4 GATT encompasses both the terms "like" and "directly competitive or substitutable" appearing in Art. III.2 GATT.

16 See GATT Doc. L/3463, adopted on 2 December 1970, BISD 18S/97.

17 The jurisprudence regarding the number of IIS digits to use in establishing likeness is unclear. The report states that the classification should be detailed enough to provide an appropriate basis. This suggests classifications below the 6-digit level would probably not qualify.

18 Henrik Horn, "National Treatment in the GATT," *American Economic Review* 96, no. 1 (2006): 394–404 constructs a two-country, two-product example whereby country A by raising, say, its consumption tax on item *b* that it does not produce (but which is of export interest to country B) in a non-discriminatory manner, might persuade country B to negotiate its current high level of consumption tax on item *a* that B does not produce but is of export interest to A.

19 Art. XVIII GATT (infant industry) is accepted in case law as an exception to, say, Art. XI GATT, hence a complainant will have to show violation of Art. XI GATT only. The burden of proof will then shift to the defendant, who will be called to justify the deviation, under Art. XVIII GATT. There

is no case law under Art. XXVIII GATT (renegotiation). A complainant attacking any of the other three instruments cannot limit its arguments to a violation of a default rule; it will have to show a violation of a provision (at the very least) of one of those instruments.

20 According to Art. VI.1 GATT, dumping is to be condemned. The WTO AB has referred to it as *"unfair trade practice."* However, nowhere does the WTO Agreement sanction dumping. Indeed, the only permissible response to dumping is, as *per* Art. 18.1 AD, the imposition of antidumping duties. Moreover, it would be quite odd for the WTO to sanction dumping, since the WTO is a government-to-government contract, whereas dumping is a purely private practice. Logically, the WTO is concerned with the only government activity in this context, that is, the imposition of duties.

21 Some countries have legislation that limits AD duties to what is needed to offset the injury caused to domestic competitors. Estimated dumping margins are often much higher than injury margins.

22 Antitrust analysis and practice (at least on both sides of the Atlantic) do not discipline price discrimination ("dumping") unless it constitutes predation – a deliberate strategy to price competitors out of the market with a view to recouping losses once all others have been forced to exit the market. Successful predation amounts to injury to competition and is thus subject to (illegal under) competition law, making AD redundant.

23 A third category, non-actionable subsidies, which comprised environmental, Research and Development, and regional subsidies lapsed in 2001 by virtue of Art. 31 SCM.

24 Assuming they prevail before the WTO adjudicating bodies, and they face a recalcitrant state, they will have to choose between CVDs and counter-measures, as noted above.

25 The SGA explicitly outlaws VERs (Art. 11). VERs were already illegal under GATT as they violated Arts. XI and Art. XIX GATT. A footnote to Art. 11 SGA creates a bit of ambiguity in that it allows foreign exporters to administer QRs. This looks very much like a VER.

26 See Alan Sykes, "The Safeguards Mess: A Critique of WTO Jurisprudence," John M. Olin Law and Economics Working Paper No. 187 (2D Series) (Chicago, IL: University of Chicago Law School, 2003).

27 Petros C. Mavroidis, *The GATT: A Commentary* (Oxford: Oxford University Press, 2005) takes the view that response should never be on an MFN basis and that *any* WTO Member can in principle respond, including those without INR or principal supplier status.

28 The Appellate Body report on *Korea – Measures Affecting Imports of Fresh, Chilled and Frozen Beef* (WTO Doc. WT/DS161 and 169/AB/R of 11 December 2000) understands "necessary" as a benchmark closer to "indispensable" rather than to "making a contribution to" but dissociates it from indispensable measures (§ 161). The same report also makes it clear that for a WTO Member to be obliged to use a less restrictive measure than the one chosen, it must not be a hypothetical, but one that is reasonably available to the intervening Member (§ 166 of the report, op. cit.).

29 The title of Art. XXI GATT (Security Exception) leaves no room to doubt that the party invoking this provision has the burden of proving it.

30 The US invoked Art. XXI GATT to justify trade measures against Cuba under the *Helms–Burton Act.* Cuba did not formally request the establish-

ment of a panel, but the EC did. The two WTO Members settled the issue during consultations.

31 Compare the standard of review applied by the European Court of Justice in re: *Commission vs. Greece* C-120/942.

32 Not all of the instruments discussed here qualify as state contingencies. Some could qualify as such, and some not. We treat them all together in this section, in order to avoid a continuous cross-referenceing across the book.

33 For extensive discussions of the WTO practice on this score, see the chapter on Preferential Trade Agreements in Petros C. Mavroidis, Robert Howse and George Bermann, *The WTO: Texts, Cases and Materials* (Eagan, MN: West Publishing, 2006).

34 André Sapir, "The Political Economy of EC Regionalism," *European Economic Review* 42, no. 3 (1998): 717–32.

35 The EC should be credited with being the origin of a substantial percentage of the first flood of PTAs. After the mid-1980s, the US followed suit.

36 See Nuno Limão, "Preferential vs. Multilateral Trade Liberalization: Evidence and Open Questions," *World Trade Review*, 5(2) (2006): 155–76.

37 On the wider issue, why many developing countries lagged in integration, see Robert E. Hudec, *Developing Countries in the GATT Legal System* (London: Gower, 1987) and Constantine Michalopoulos, *Developing Countries in the WTO* (Basingstoke: Palgrave, 2001).

38 Although, in principle, legal challenges against such invocations are not excluded outright, nothing of the sort has so far happened in the GATT/WTO.

39 A decision to grant a waiver in respect of any obligation subject to a transition period or a period for staged implementation that the requesting Member has not performed by the end of the relevant period shall be taken only by consensus.

4 Services and intellectual property

1 This reading of the term "none" has been confirmed by the panel in § 6.279 of its report on *US – Gambling*.

2 The 2001 replaced the 1993 Scheduling Guidelines.

3 The first of these two categories can be discarded since in such cases WTO Members will simply introduce the term *unbound*. If liberalization of the service concerned eventually becomes technically feasible, new negotiations will have to take place to define the level of commitment. The second category (*special cases*) is in practice merged with the category *commitment with limitations*.

4 Subparagraph 2(c) does not cover measures of a Member which limit inputs for the supply of services.

5 Some WTO Members had privatized their telecoms operators prior to the GATS negotiation. An institutional vehicle was thus required to ensure that through a government-to-government contract, private parties would be effectively compelled to adopt a particular behavior (reasonable, cost-based, access pricing, that is, interconnection rates). The Reference Paper is the institutional vehicle designed by the negotiators to fill this vacuum.

6 Art. XX.2 GATS does not seem to contradict this construction: according to this provision only measures *inconsistent* with both Art. XVI and XVII GATS will have to appear under the column "Art. XVI GATS." Assuming the more onerous market access treatment is expressed through mechanisms

other than those reflected in Art. XVI GATS, governments will indicate in Art. XVII GATS what the limitations on national treatment consist of.

7 Assuming this view of Art. XVI GATS is accepted, some schedules of concession would have to be re-evaluated, since some of them reflect *non-discriminatory* (i.e., applicable to both domestic and foreign suppliers) limitations. This is probably the result of the highly confusing *1993 Scheduling Guidelines.*

8 Albeit with modifications or extensions in some cases, e.g., the Art. 6 *bis* Berne Convention provision on moral rights, with respect to which WTO Members have no rights and incur no obligations.

9 The TRIPs Agreement requires that persons lawfully controlling trade secrets or know-how of commercial value be protected from the trade secrets at hand being disseminated without their consent.

10 For the purposes of this Article, the terms "inventive step" and "capable of industrial application" may be deemed by a Member to be synonymous with the terms "non-obvious" and "useful" respectively.

11 This right, like all other rights conferred under this Agreement in respect of the use, sale, importation or other distribution of goods, is subject to the provisions of Article 6.

5 Dispute settlement, transparency, and plurilateral agreements

1 On the procedural aspects of the WTO dispute settlement system, see David N. Palmeter and Petros C. Mavroidis, *Dispute Settlement in the WTO: Practice and Procedure*, 2nd edition (Cambridge: Cambridge University Press, 2004).

2 Hudec acknowledges that information on this is incomplete. Robert E. Hudec, *Enforcing International Trade Law* (London: Butterworth, 1993).

3 Although adopted reports might not be implemented (and a losing party might refuse to acquiesce to countermeasures against it), by adopting a report, the loser accepts that the specific interpretation of the GATT is sound. Implementation of the recommendations of panel reports is distinct from acceptance of the panel's interpretation.

4 As is the case with the other subjects covered in this book, space constraints prevent a comprehensive treatment of either the case law or the policy debates surrounding the operation of the WTO dispute settlement system. See e.g., Robert Lawrence, *Crimes and Punishment: Retaliation under the WTO* (Washington, DC: Institute for International Economics, 2003) for a policy-oriented, critical analysis of the functioning of the DSU.

5 John H. Jackson, *World Trade and the Law of the GATT* (Bloomington, IN: Bobbs-Merrill, 1969) notes that although it never happened, it was legally possible for a GATT contracting party to submit a dispute to the International Court of Justice. Such a course of action would violate the letter and the spirit of the DSU under the present WTO regime.

6 William J. Davey, "Dispute Settlement in GATT," *Fordham International Law Journal* 11 (1987): 51–99 provides an excellent analysis of the distinction between judicial systems that favor adjudication as opposed to those favoring negotiation.

7 We believe that this is wrong. The DSU mentions the possibility of only one RPT. For a second compliance panel to exist, there is by construction the need to have more than one RPT.

8 On this issue, see the very insightful analysis in Robert Lawrence, *Crimes and Punishment: Retaliation under the WTO* (Washington, DC: Institute for International Economics, 2003).

9 The *Bananas* arbitration (WTO Doc. WT/DS27) casts doubt on the validity of this sentence since the Arbitrators requested the complainants to take action in sectors that the complainants themselves had envisaged no action. We believe that this opinion is contrary to the unambiguous letter and spirit of Art. 22 DSU and hopefully, this case law will be soon reversed through future practice or through legislative activity in the context of the DSU review.

10 It should be noted, however, that in cases of prohibited subsidies, affected WTO Members have been authorized to adopt countermeasures up to the level of the subsidy granted independently of the injury suffered.

11 Arguing that no equivalence can be established, the Arbitrators in the US Antidumping Act of 1916 (WTO Doc. WT/DS136/ARB of 24 February 2004) did not authorize the EC to adopt a mirror legislation to that of the US found to be WTO-inconsistent.

12 In the Doha Round negotiations, the African group of countries proposed the introduction of monetary damages, whereas Mexico proposed the introduction of tradable remedies.

13 Henrik Horn and Petros C. Mavroidis, "WTO Dispute Settlement Database" (2006), http://www.worldbank.org/trade/wtodisputes.

14 Art. X GATT is the default transparency provision in the GATT system. It should be read in conjunction with specific transparency provision embedded in agreements annexed to the GATT, to the extent that such exist.

15 Direct effect is the corresponding term to self-executing. Absent a clear and unambiguous statement to this effect in the body of an international treaty, the issue whether a provision has direct effect or not is a matter for consideration under domestic law.

16 See Bernard M. Hoekman and Michel Kostecki, *The Political Economy of the World Trading System* (Oxford: Oxford University Press, 2001) for more details.

17 Members comprise Bulgaria, Canada, Chinese Taipei, Estonia, the European Community (and its 15 members individually), Egypt, Georgia, Japan, Latvia (now an EU member), Macau, Malta (now also an EU member), Norway, Romania, Switzerland, and the United States.

18 Art. XIII.2 GATS states that multilateral negotiations on procurement of services should take place within two years from the entry into force of the WTO Agreement. The Guidelines and Procedures for the Negotiations on Trade in Services (WTO Doc. S/L/93) state that Members should complete negotiations under Art. XIII GATS before negotiating specific commitments on procurement. So far, negotiations have been inconclusive.

19 See Bernard M. Hoekman and Petros C. Mavroidis (eds) *Law and Policy in Public Purchasing* (Ann Abour, MA: University of Michigan Press, 1997).

6 Developing countries and the WTO

1 GATT, *Trends in International Trade* (Geneva: GATT, 1958).

2 The degree of homogeneity across developing countries, as understood in those years, was relatively higher in the early 1960s. It was thus easier for

them to reach consensus among them, and formulate common demands that corresponded more or less to similar needs.

3 See GATT, COM.TD/W/37, p. 9.

4 A host of countries, for example, disagreed with Korea's decision to invoke Art. XVIII GATT (only developing countries can invoke it), and not Art. XII GATT, which is reserved for use by developed countries only, when it was facing balance of payments problems.

5 Turkey has been a *sui generis* case in this respect.

6 The AB suggests that the drafters could easily have inserted the term *all* before developing countries, if they had wanted to stress that no discrimination across developing countries is permitted. Gene M. Grossman and Alan Sykes, "A Preference for Development: the Law and Economics of GSP," *World Trade Review* 4, no. 1 (2005): 41–68 take issue with this, arguing that the AB has treated silence in a very inconsistent manner in its case law. They argue that, by the same token, the drafters could have inserted the term *certain* before developing countries, if they wanted to allow for discrimination. The fact that they did not is probably equally relevant in understanding their intent. They take the view that based not on silence, but on actual expression, the Enabling Clause makes one distinction only: between developing and least developed countries.

7 This is still debated. See, for example, Grossman and Sykes, "A Preference for Development"; Bernard Hoekman, "Operationalizing the Concept of Policy Space in the WTO: Beyond Special and Differential Treatment," *Journal of International Economic Law* 8, no. 2 (2005): 405–24; Dani Rodrik, "What is Wrong with the (Augmented) Washington Consensus?" (2002) mimeo. www.sopde.org/discussion.htm; and, Christopher Stevens, "The Future of SDT for Developing Countries in the WTO," Institute for Development Studies, Sussex (mimeo. May 2002).

8 On this point, see the analysis in Grossman and Sykes, "A Preference for development," 41–68.

9 The calculation was done at the HS 8-digit level. There are 10,500 8-digit tariff lines.

7 Whither the trading system after Doha? Deadlock as an opportunity?

1 See Keith Maskus, *Intellectual Property Rights in the Global Economy* (Washington, DC: Institute of International Economics, 2000).

2 Of course, no generalizations are possible here – much depends at the household level on whether people are net consumers or producers, and on the relative size of income versus consumption impacts of policies.

3 The data in this paragraph are taken from Patrick Messerlin, "Reforming Agricultural Policies in the Doha Round," in Simon Evenett and Bernard Hoekman (eds) *Economic Development and Multilateral Cooperation* (London: Palgrave Macmillan and World Bank, 2006), 3–40.

4 These examples are drawn from M. Ataman Aksoy and John Beghin (eds) *Global Agricultural Trade and Developing Countries* (Washington, DC: World Bank, 2005).

5 See, for example, Joseph Francois, Bernard Hoekman and Miriam Manchin, "Preference Erosion and Multilateral Trade Liberalization," *World Bank Economic Review* 20, no. 2 (2006): 197–216, and the references cited there.

6 The CRTA has proven to be quite ineffective in enforcing the relevant WTO rules. As noted in Chapter 3, not much should be expected of efforts to strengthen enforcement of WTO rules for PTAs – past history has made it abundantly clear that this was not acceptable to major players in the past. Moreover, it would seem somewhat hypocritical to propose to start enforcing existing rules now that the EU appears increasingly able to comply with them.

7 See Susan Prowse, "Aid for Trade – Increasing Support for Trade Adjustment and Integration: A Proposal," in *Economic Development and Multilateral Cooperation*, ed. Simon Evenett and Bernard Hoekman (London: Palgrave Macmillan and World Bank, 2006), 229–68, for a detailed discussion of the rationale for, and possible modalities of, "aid for trade."

8 Any multilateral trade liberalization can be expected to generate sizeable net gains to both industrialized and developing countries. The overall magnitude of such gains is difficult to assess accurately – much depends on what is agreed and how it is implemented, but even conservative estimates of the aggregate global gains are significant. In absolute terms, high-income countries will gain more than developing countries, providing the means to engage in increased support and development assistance.

9 See Michael J. Finger, *The Doha Agenda and Development: A View from the Uruguay Round* (Manila: Asian Development Bank, 2002) and Michael J. Finger and Philip Schuler, "Implementation of Uruguay Round Commitments: The Development Challenge," *World Economy* 23, no. 4 (2000): 511–26.

10 The group was formed pre-Cancún. It included Argentina, Bolivia, Brazil, Chile, China, Colombia, Costa Rica, Cuba, Ecuador, El Salvador, Guatemala, India, Mexico, Pakistan, Paraguay, Peru, the Philippines, South Africa, Thailand and Venezuela. Over time membership has changed, but the name was kept as G-20.

11 In practice, small and poor countries are unlikely to impose serious externalities on large countries. However, actions even by LDCs may have significant effects on neighboring poor countries.

12 There is an emerging literature that argues in favor of a "learning" approach to international cooperation in complex regulation-intensive domestic policy domains. For example, Abram Chayes and Antonia Handler Chayes, *The New Sovereignty: Compliance with International Regulatory Agreements* (Cambridge, MA: Harvard University Press, 1995), and Dani Rodrik, "What is Wrong with the (Augmented) Washington Consensus?" (2002) mimeo. www.sopde.org/discussion.htm. Bernard Hoekman applies some of these insights to the subject of differential treatment for developing countries in the WTO in "Operationalizing the Concept of Policy Space in the WTO: Beyond Special and Differential Treatment," *Journal of International Economic Law* 8, no. 2 (2005): 405–24.

Select bibliography

There is a huge literature on the WTO from different perspectives: historical, economic, political science, international relations and legal. Douglas Irwin, *Free Trade Under Fire* (Princeton, NJ: Princeton University Press, 2005) discusses the history of the GATT and the influence that the United States has had on the advent of the multilateral trading system. For detailed appraisals and a history of the negotiations of the Havana Charter and the General Agreement on Tariffs and Trade, see William Brown, *The United States and the Restoration of World Trade* (Washington, DC: The Brookings Institution, 1950) and William Diebold, *The End of the ITO* (Princeton, NJ: Princeton University Press, 1952).

John H. Jackson's classic book, *World Trade and the Law of the GATT* (Bloomington, IN: Bobbs-Merrill, 1969) is the starting point for an in-depth treatment of the legal intricacies of the GATT. Mitsuo Matsushita, Thomas J. Schonbaum and Petros C. Mavroidis, *The World Trade Organization, Law, Practice, and Policy* (Oxford: Oxford University Press, 2nd edition, 2006) offer a comprehensive legal analysis of all WTO covered agreements. Robert E. Hudec, *The GATT Legal System and the World Trade Diplomacy* (New York: Praeger, 1975) is a classic analysis of the GATT's design and its first 30 years.

The economics of the trading system's rules and disciplines are assessed in Bernard Hoekman and Michel Kostecki, *The Political Economy of the World Trading System* (Oxford: Oxford University Press, 2001). Amrita Narlikar, *The WTO: A Very Short Introduction* (Oxford: Oxford University Press, 2005), is an up-to-date treatment of the WTO that focuses on the politics of the organization. For short introductions to the content and economics of many of the subjects covered by – or proposed for – the WTO, see the contributions in Bernard Hoekman, Aaditya Mattoo and Philip English, eds., *Development, Trade and the WTO: A Handbook* (Washington, DC: The World Bank, 2002).

John Odell (ed.) *Negotiating Trade: Developing Countries in the WTO and NAFTA* (Cambridge: Cambridge University Press, 2006) is a collection of studies and cases that focus on the process of negotiations and the strategies that have been used by developing countries. Maurice Schiff and L. A. Winters,

Regionalism and Development (Oxford: Oxford University Press, 2003) is a book-length treatment of the economics of preferential trade, accessible to non-economists and including an analysis of the politics of regionalism. Priorities and alternative options to extend the GATS are the subject of papers collected in Pierre Sauvé and Robert Stern (eds) *GATS 2000: New Directions in Services Trade Liberalization* (Washington, DC: Brookings Institution, 2000). Keith Maskus, *Intellectual Property Rights in the Global Economy* (Washington, DC: Institute for International Economics, 2000) is a highly recommended book-length survey and analysis of the economic implications of the TRIPs agreement. Alan O. Sykes, "The Safeguards Mess: A Critique of WTO Jurisprudence," *World Trade Review* 3 (2003): 216–96 explains how an imprecise legal text coupled with sloppy interpretations has resulted in an impossible legal test for governments interested in using this instrument.

WTO dispute settlement procedures are discussed in detail by David Palmeter and Petros C. Mavroidis, *Dispute Settlement in the World Trade Organization: Practice and Procedure* (The Hague: Kluwer Law International, 1999). Robert Lawrence, *Crimes and Punishments: Retaliation under the WTO* (Washington, DC: Institute for International Economics, 2003) discusses the experience with and alternative options for improving the DSU. Claude Barfield, *Free Trade, Sovereignty, Democracy: The Future of the World Trade Organization* (Washington, DC: American Enterprise Institute, 2001) analyzes the structural features of the WTO dispute resolution system and argues there is an imbalance between the (efficient) judicial arm of the WTO and its (inefficient and unwieldy) legislative/rule-making arm and discusses the option of introducing "soft law" as a possible principle to be utilized in WTO dispute settlements.

Jagdish Bhagwati and Robert Hudec (eds) *Harmonization and Fair Trade: Prerequisite for Free Trade?* (Cambridge, MA: MIT Press, 1996) offer an inter-disciplinary discussion of the challenges of deeper integration and the problems of dealing with domestic policy differences through international cooperation. Steve Charnovitz, "The WTO and Cosmopolitics," *Journal of International Economic Law* 7, no. 3 (2004): 675–82 discusses the WTO's relationship with civil society. In the same issue, James Bacchus, a former US Congressman and Appellate Body judge, and Julio Lacarte, a senior Uruguayan trade official and also an ex-chair of the Appellate Body, provide a "WTO view" on matters related to transparency and participation.

John H. Jackson, in *Sovereignty, the WTO, and Changing Fundamentals of International Law* (Cambridge: Cambridge University Press, 2006) offers a comprehensive outlook on the modern challenges to national sovereignty.

Websites

www.wto.org: The WTO home page.
www.worldtradelaw.net: Currently the best WTO portal available. Includes a links section: www.worldtradelaw.net/miscella.htm

www.cid.harvard.edu/cidtrade: The Global Trade Negotiations homepage, maintained by the Center for International Development (Harvard University). Compiles recent research from a variety of sources on trade negotiations and economic development.

www.ictsd.org: International Centre for Trade and Sustainable Development. Publishes the newsletter *Bridges* as well as *Trade Negotiation Insights*. One of the best sources of information and analysis of developments on the trade negotiation front.

www.unctad.org/Templates/Page.asp?intItemID=2741: An UNCTAD course on dispute resolution

www.worldbank.org/research/trade/index.htm: World Bank International Trade site, includes numerous downloadable papers on a variety of trade policy topics, including WTO agreements and negotiations.

www.insidetrade.com: Daily news and analysis of trade-related developments, including WTO and regional trade negotiations

http://finance.groups.yahoo.com/group/wto_forum: Yahoo! WTO Forum

www.worldbank.org/trade/wtodisputes: Database of all WTO disputes from 1995–2005.

Index

GLOBAL INSTITUTIONS SERIES

NEW TITLE
United Nations Conference on Trade and Development (UNCTAD)

Ian Taylor, University of St Andrews, UK and
Karen Smith, University of Stellenbosch, South Africa

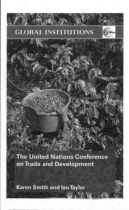

A much-needed new examination of the United Nations Conference on Trade and Development (UNCTAD), fully covering its history and current activities. Ian Taylor and Karen Smith present a clear overview to an organization that is at times overlooked and seen to belong to a bygone era. All the key areas are covered by accessibly written chapters.

Contents
Introduction 1. Historical background 2. UNCTAD's secretariat structure 3. Research, analysis and major publications 4. "Golden years," 1960s–1970s 5. Crisis, retreat and reinvention, 1980s–onwards 6. The multilateral trading system and the future: where does UNCTAD fit into the WTO? 7. Conclusion

May 2007: 216x138mm: 152pp
Hb: 978–0–415–37020–2: **£65.00**
Pb: 978–0–415–37019–6: **£14.99**

NEW TITLE
A Crisis in Global Institutions?
Multilateralism and international security

Edward Newman, United Nations University, Tokyo

This volume considers if there is a crisis in global institutions which address security challenges, exploring the sources of these challenges and how multilateralism might be more viably constituted to cope with contemporary and future demands.

Contents
1. Introduction 2. Defining the crisis of multilateralism in the area of international peace and security 3. Sources of the crisis of multilateralism 4. Emerging alternatives to the existing values and institutions of multilateralism 5. New multilateralism? Towards a "post-Westphalian" model of multilateralism 6. Conclusion

June 2007: 234x156: 184pp
Hb: 978–0–415–41164–6: **£65.00**
Pb: 978–0–415–41165–3: **£16.99**

Routledge
Taylor & Francis Group

To order any of these titles
Call: +44 (0) 1264 34 3071
Fax: +44 (0) 1264 34 3005
Email: book.orders@routledge.co.uk

For further information visit:
www.routledge.com/politics